T0313427

"The nature of business is changing, and organizations experience the need to change accordingly. In this book, Jan-Jacob Koomen takes the reader on a fascinating journey, revealing how firms can successfully adapt to and become part of the new market reality. Using exciting insights from nature as metaphors, he discusses why and how firms need to re-invent themselves in today's increasingly interconnected world. The book provides the reader with insightful and ready-to-apply ideas, concepts, and frameworks in a unique, storytelling way. As such, the book empowers and inspires at the same time. I highly recommend it to managers of medium-sized firms seeking to grow their business and create value for its stakeholders."
– Ruud Frambach, Professor of Marketing, Vrije Universiteit Amsterdam

"It is an excellent read for start-ups that want to evolve into scale-ups, and companies wanting to co-operate with such scale-ups."
– Auke van de Hout, Managing Partner Graduate Entrepreneur

"An interesting book that introduces the concept of the platform company and explains how to be successful in a highly dynamic and unpredictable world."
– Quintin Schevernels, Consigliere for start- and scale-ups, Serial Entrepreneur and Former CEO of Funda and Layar

"*The Platform Company* provides great insights that can accelerate modern strategy formation in corporations. It takes you out of the comfort zone, and forces you into a tough evaluation of the competitive position of the organization."
– Eric van Westbroek, Director Consumer & Online PostNL, Managing Director Innovation Studio PostNL

The Platform Company

*The Art of Resilient Strategy: A Guide for Leaders
Inspired by Nature's Competition*

Jan-Jacob Koomen

Amsterdam University Press

Also check out the companion website: https://platformcompany.net

Cover design: Gijs Mathijs Ontwerpers
Lay-out: Crius Group, Hulshout

ISBN	978 90 4855 967 1
e-ISBN	978 90 4855 968 8
DOI	10.5117/9789048559671
NUR	801

Printed and bound by CPI Group (UK) Ltd, Croydon, CR0 4YY

Table of Contents

Preface

As a leader, you may be facing challenges in determining the most appropriate course of action for your company or organization amid current uncertainty. The Platform Company approach will help you address these challenges, give clear guidance on how to make you organization more resilient and significantly increase your ability to influence your success.

Digitalization has sped up the innovation cycle and disrupts existing business models. As a result, the dynamism in the current business environment has grown for many years.

More recently, global issues, such the climate, demographics, Covid, and the rebalancing of power between countries are driving more unpredictable and stronger interventions from governments leading to accelerated dynamism.

To address the increased dynamism, the way companies do strategy needs an update from the old paradigm, which has a strong focus on those aspects that are owned or appear directly in the top or bottom line.

Instead, the focus should be on all aspects that drive the value chain of a company or organization, all those aspects that, ultimately, affect the ability to create value for the end customer.

One way to do this is through the platform company approach. This helps companies be more responsive and consider the whole ecosystem they are working in. The platform company approach will give your organization a competitive advantage and increase its chances of success in today's dynamic business landscape.

The platform company approach can help you plan your strategy and make your company more responsive. It is a useful tool for all leaders to have.

The book uses examples from nature that encourage thinking beyond set paradigms. Nature is a very long running experiment on competitive strategy, and the study of ecology provides many examples and models that are helpful for modern leaders.

I hope the book inspires you. I hope it provides enough structure and concrete action-oriented activities, as well as stimulating the quest for deeper understanding of what drives success and survival in business. I hope it offers enough insights into ecology, without losing the competitive strategy focus.

Structure of the book

The book investigates the platform strategy in multiple ways: as a set of ideas inspired by nature and ecology; as a strategic model; and as step-by-step approach. The platform concept is explored as the story of Jack, a CEO on safari in Africa. In the six days of his trip, he covers six aspects of the platform strategy:

1 **Brands:** How brands can be adapted in a digitally connected social space, and how to get traction in brand value creation.
2 **Sales channels:** How to analyze the end customer buying process and find ways to navigate distribution and channel conflicts.
3 **Innovation:** How to understand the impact of uncertainty on innovation and optimize collaboration to differentiate.
4 **Value leadership:** How to find value for end customers and design a competitive platform to deliver.
5 **Strategy:** How to bring the platform together as a strategy and how business environment determines design.
6 **Leadership:** Determine the key battle to pick as a leader of the transformation.

The story is about a company (Matthew &Sons (M&S)) that creates products. It is used as an example to explain some more specific aspects of the method. The exact M&S proposition is not made clear in order to accentuate the generalist nature of the method. The method also applies to companies that provide services and to non-commercial organizations.

Each chapter starts with an issue that arises in Jack's company. The issue is then investigated using various experiences on his safari trip. Concepts from nature and ecology are used to introduce the right paradigm. At the end of each chapter, Jack draws the necessary conclusions and mails his findings and the next steps to his team in the United States. The emails at the end of each chapter tell both the whole story of platform strategy and the practical steps you can take to use this method for your organization.

Many chapters contain examples from nature and ecology to explain platform strategy concepts outside the box. These 'Lessons from nature' are marked and can be read for interest and inspiration. They can also be scanned. The main conclusion for business is always given at the end of such an intermezzo. The presented theory is not scientific rigorous, but rather simplified to better convey the message.

Introduction:
The start of the six-day journey

Fig Tree camp was no ordinary camp. As the plane descended slowly toward the airstrip on the Kenyan savannah and the familiar contours of trees on the banks of Talek River became clearer, Jack started to distinguish the herds of topi antelopes and zebra on the plains and welcomed the warm and invigorating energy that this tented camp always gave him.

He was looking forward to a six-day safari and realized that, unlike many previous trips, he would not be able to unwind as much as he would like to. Since his visit last year, his fourth-generation family business had experienced a series of setbacks, disappointing results, and failures. It had probably been one of the worst years in the 115 years of Matthews & Sons' existence.

Even in the recession some years ago, the business had managed to remain successful, by sourcing lower cost parts, reducing manufacturing costs, and ramping up promotional activity. But now, somehow, this recipe had run out of steam.

He had hesitated to go on this trip at all, but Suzi, his daughter, convinced him that six days away from the office would not make a difference. She suggested that maybe a break would help him clear his mind and come up with fresh thinking and new ideas.

The plane touched down and he was greeted by the staff and the vehicle of the Fig Tree Camp. In the coming week, Jack would have ample time to contemplate his business, under the shade of the fig vines, and ponder the future of the industry, overlooking the herds on the immense plains. The savannah gave him an opportunity to take a step back and dive into a familiar world of the African plains, rather than his day-to-day struggle with urgent challenges such as social advertising, data-driven business, climate neutral commuting, Artificial Intelligence, ChatGPT and all the other new concepts that were landing on his desk on a daily basis.

He took his laptop bag from the seat, helped his wife, Caroline, step out of the small plane, and greeted Mike, their guide for the coming days.

After they had settled into their tented rooms, they met other guests at dinner but they did not hang around long as they were tired from their trip.

News from the home front: Diminishing impact of advertising

Back at the tent, Jack and Caroline opened their laptops to check their mail before going to bed.

The news was not positive. Nancy O' Connell, the Marketing VP, had forwarded him the review of the most recent marketing campaign and the results were disappointing.

Jack resolved to spend some time on it the following day. As he closed his laptop, the sounds of the African night pulled him into a deep, restful sleep.

1.   Utilitarian brands: Reimagining brand value creation in a connected audience

Competing birds – The handicap principle shows how transparency creates trust

Jack and Caroline were savoring the crisp, chilly morning in the Masai Mara with a cup of tea. They had opted to skip the early morning drive and planned to join a trip to a buffalo herd later in the day. Jack noticed one of the Masai guards slowly walking toward a bush near the next tent. He was looking intently at a scene of two beautiful birds, male grenadier finches, which were trying to attract the attention of a third, much duller female bird. The males were conspicuously colored in shades of purple and held a small stem in their bill.

'These birds are so taken up by their courtship that we can have a close look without disturbing them,' whispered the guide.

The female finch was intently assessing the quality of both males, choosing the father of her future offspring wisely. She took her time, as the quality of her nestlings would depend heavily on the choice of mate. She was likely looking for qualities such as fitness, resistance to diseases, as well as the potential of her offspring to attract future mates and propagate her genes.

How could one male convince the female that he has superior qualities compared to the other? Surely any old finch could start waving stems at a potential partner, but how would that demonstrate his quality to her. How could his message become trustworthy?

The guard whispered: 'She will select the left male.' Sure enough, a few minutes later, the male on the left flew off with his prize.

'How did you know?' Jack asked.

The guard explained: 'The other one on the right is slightly brighter, but thinner. The bright colors are a burden to him in his day-to-day struggle for survival, as he cannot support to be so conspicuous and stay fat at the same time. The bird on the left shows that, even with the handicap of the bright colors, he can survive in good health. He must be really fit. It's always the ones with the combination of bright colors and healthy appearance that win. They call this the Handicap Principle.'

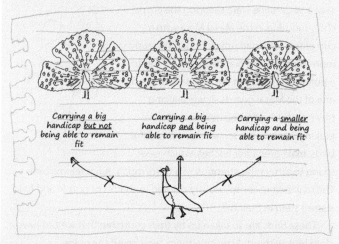

Figure 1.1: Handicap principle: A message is more trustworthy if it carries a heavy cost. Only the fittest peacocks can squander resources on the tail and remain healthy.

How the Handicap principle is a common phenomenon to make a message more trustworthy

This is why Jack loved Africa so much. Waking up every day with beautiful scenes of nature on the doorstep of your tent. He pondered the issue of using a handicap to build trust in a message and how this could apply to business. He remembered the case of a famous brand from the early days of marketing: Sunlight soap.

A century ago, one of Unilever's founders, Lord Lever, used a handicap to build trust with consumers. He wrapped his soap in distinctive packaging, so that consumers could easily recognize it as coming from his factory. Today, this hardly seems a handicap, but at the time many producers could earn high profits by cutting corners and tinkering with the quality of their products as long as they got away with it. In such an environment, a recognizable product is a huge handicap for a company intent on fiddling with the quality of the soap. A poorly performing box of soap with a recognizable brand on it would instantly discourage consumers from purchasing any similarly branded products in future. 'Surely any producer that would make his soap recognizable, and stay in business, needs to provide reasonable quality soap'. The success of the Lever brothers shows that this concept was very effective.

Even this early form of marketing communication worked with the handicap principle! 'What about that!' Jack was excited by this insight as he focused on further exploring this line of thought.

He now realized that the handicap principle was driving human behavior all around him:

- An expensive race car communicates financial success quite effectively. It is not just the price that matters. To truly communicate financial success, the car needs to be both expensive and impractical. In that way, it forms a real financial handicap, a burden that only successful people can afford.
- Someone who queues for 48 hours to get the first iPhone pays the same price as a consumer who buys the phone a few weeks later. However, the first day iPhone transfers the handicap not by price but by the trouble taken to acquire one.
- In the past, when most people still did manual labor, a tie was a significant handicap. Wearing is a reliable way of communicating that you earn your living without doing any dirty work. Doing business in the '80s, if you could be successful without wearing a tie, or even while wearing a turtleneck, you demonstrated your ability to achieve despite

this handicap, thus signaling your power or potential. Today, as desk work is not very exclusive, the tie has lost its shine.
– The growth of products or services that require buyer participation is another example. For instance, sustainable veg box subscriptions that expect the customer to help out on the land, or mobile subscriptions such as Giff-Gaff where users are invited to support to each other. These are all great choices to show your dedication to a lifestyle that values the environment and other people.

Jack concluded that a handicap is frequently used in evaluating the trustworthiness of a message.

Corollary 1: Messages can be made trustworthy if the sender adds a 'handicap' to the message, such that a false message would inflict costs that are difficult to conceal. This is known as the handicap principle.

Many other examples came to mind, including some companies that had built a trusted brand by repeating their brand values on TV. Jack realized that, nowadays, any firm could create a branded product and buy advertising space on TV. Even as TV audiences decrease, by going multi-channel, firms can still attract a sufficient number of viewers for their message. However, as the recent experience of M&S showed, expanding the media push does not always result in end customer conviction or trust in the brand. And he certainly could not spend the sums of money required to create a presence that would stand out, like the large brands adverting during Super Bowl.

How pushing a message harder on multiple channels is counterproductive if it is falsifiable

Jack decided to use his moment of inspiration to address the disappointing results of the campaign mentioned in Nancy's email.
Nancy was hired eight months ago from a sports drink company where she had been responsible for a successful multi-channel

campaign for the US Open. Nancy had been hired specifically to modernize the company's marketing efforts through her expertise in online social advertising.

Nancy convinced Jack to invest in updating the brand with a new payoff that supported a premium, high-quality positioning of Matthews & Sons. She concentrated 45 per cent of the annual budget on the new campaign to allow for a sufficiently large media burst, covering a range of channels.

The agency had developed artwork that resonated with the M&S employees. The staff had responded very positively and experienced a morale boost due to the modern approach, the funny commercials, and the slick video content.

However, the result had barely lifted the top line. In an effort to boost sales, the campaign was adjusted to include more aggressive promotions and discounting some of the lesser products, whilst maintaining margin on the core.

After the first disappointing sales results came in, Jack had convinced himself that the campaigns just needed some time to gain traction. He hoped that the results would start to emerge over time. He had asked for a report that shed light on what was happening with the thoughts and behaviors of their end customers, in order to distinguish those aspects of the campaign that could be improved.

As he anxiously processed Nancy's report, Jack's doubts exacerbated rather than alleviated.

The campaign had been successful in terms of reaching the audience, and the 'helped recognition' of the new slogan was above expectation. However, the impact on end customers' attitude to M&S had hardly budged. In fact, the perception of quality had even deteriorated slightly.

M&S had not been able to gain their end customers' trust in the message it sent.

After the experience with the grenadier finches, Jack wondered: 'Could the handicap principle be of use to create trust for M&S? If so, what is the modern handicap that M&S could chase? What handicap will gain trust with end customers?'

Jack reviewed the company message and realized that by just adding channels to the media mix, M&S was completely missing this point of trust. Choosing additional social channels pushes the message further into the life of end customers; it increases reach. At the same time, however, it exposes the message to falsification and risks deterioration of trust.

In the digital age, end customers are more informed and empowered to verify the message much more widely. Pushing harder only strengthens mistrust in the message if it is not supported by other sources of customer information.

Jack decided to check this out for himself. In the last few weeks, the marketing department regularly forwarded links to M&S's online promotions. Now, Jack conducted a Google search for M&S. He felt sure that the M&S advertisement link would be the first result, but instead the highest unpaid link was an 'anti-slavery forum'. This was a website where end customers discussed the employment conditions at overseas production facilities. M&S featured prominently in the discussion. A few weeks ago, the PR department had briefed Jack on the public discussion related to this subject, which included M&S. He now realized that anyone who was looking up M&S would get this message, supported by comments of many fellow end customers. This was not strengthening an image of quality.

He clicked on the next link, a blog came up called 'Homeguru', where M&S products featured in several chat streams. He read a few. Although comments on M&S products were generally good, the overall tone was not positive. There were many comments about unclear installation instructions. Even worse were the comments on experiences with the customer service department. Some customers complained about the fact that they had bought a discounted product but later discovered that the discounts in a subsequent campaign were even higher. Jack felt disgusted: 'What do the people expect? That we give away these products for free? When will they appreciate how big a hit we have taken in our margin to accommodate these promotions?'

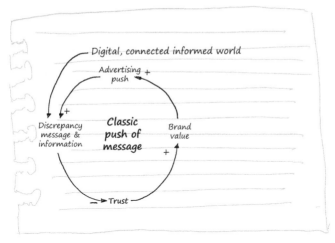

Figure 1.2: Decreasing potential of pushing messages in an informed world.

All the examples had one thing in common: they created a discrepancy between what M&S wanted to convey in its message and the end customers' perception of M&S.

He made a small sketch in an old-fashioned notebook he had collected at the reception of the lodge.

How the digital age creates opportunities for falsifiable messages that create trust

He opened the site of OutdoorKings, a distributor of high-end products that often need require professional installation. To his surprise, the OutdoorKings website opened on a page with a big interview on SunnyFountain, a small upstart competitor. The interview hardly mentioned the products of SunnyFountain (which were of inferior quality) but spent many paragraphs on the corporate culture of this upstart, in particular the way they aligned it with the product brand values.

He investigated the online presence of SunnyFountain a bit further. He found a wealth of information on the company, including details on their manufacturing process, and even some links to their Vietnamese sourcing. Jack forwarded some of the links

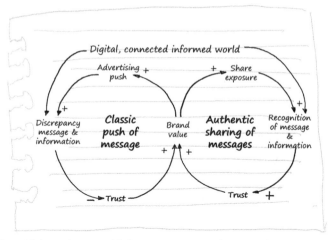

Figure 1.3: Increasing potential of transparency in an informed world.

to Frances Snyder, who was heading M&S strategic analysis, including competitor analysis. They would have a field day with the lack of control on SunnyFountain information.

Jack browsed back to Homeguru and looked for any references to SunnyFountain. Any joy about his espionage achievements quickly disappeared. To his amazement, he found many positive stories about SunnyFountain there. How was this possible? They loved the stories the company was sharing, even if most of them had never read the original publications. 'Customers had a higher confidence with an inferior product, just because they liked the way the staff dressed? Because it promised an "easy life"?'

'Would anyone believe this story?' Jack said aloud. Then he realized that the audience did believe it. They have every reason to trust it, precisely because the transparency on SunnyFountain creates the trust, much like the recognizable packaging of the sunlight soap.

SunnyFountain not only conveyed an 'easy life' message, but also shared a lot of information to the end customer to validate this message. The real proof of the genuineness of the message was that the company was 'easy' in the way it was run. It sacrificed efficiency for the benefit of ease.

Moreover, SunnyFountain was leveraging the communication of others to strengthen this trust; not exactly pushing it, but rather enabling others to join a platform for open exchange that was carefully crafted through stories about the way the company behaves and the experiences around using their products. In addition to strengthening trust, this also creates a sense of security that a customer's choice will get the thumbs up from a peer group that is slightly aspirational for that customer.

Jack expanded his drawing on his notepad to include the SunnyFountain approach.

Corollary 2: Transparency is an excellent way to create trust, as it creates a handicap for the firm on every false message it sends.

Buying binoculars: The objective of brands is utilitarian value

Jack was brought back to reality as
Mike arrived to pick them up for the
game drive. He was soon drawn into
the spectacle of the African plains
instead.

They drove over to a spot where
a large herd of Cape buffalo had
been reported. The jeep stopped at a
respectable distance. Jack took out his new binoculars to look at the
crowded dusty detail of the herds, holding his gaze for some time
on a huge male that was destroying some of the shrubs by digging
them up with his horns, for no apparent reason. He was glad that
the guides always kept a safe distance from these beasts.

As he lowered his binoculars, his eyes were caught by the sophisticated small red logo on the right side of the binoculars' casing. He
had recently bought this new pair. Now, as he used them to survey
his surroundings, he could not recall exactly why he had selected
this particular pair, but the realization that he had bought a top
brand felt reassuring.

His thoughts drifted back to the outdoor store where he had pur-
chased them. He had been overwhelmed by the vast selection, a wall
of over eight meters, filled with binoculars of all sizes and shapes.
The breadth of the assortment was far too big, even if he had taken
the time to study the range online at home beforehand, comparing
detailed lists of the binoculars' different features, which he had not.

He had narrowed his choices down to three brands, which he
knew were well regarded. He had placed a high-end model of each
brand on the counter. Each was a good-quality product.

He compared the three items: For one brand he remembered an
advertisement showing a funky youngster on a rooftop in Manhat-
tan, using the binoculars to spot a girl three blocks away, certainly
not the kind of association he welcomed. By contrast, he associated
the other two with adventurous images in the wild.

As he considered the remaining two options, he imagined himself walking through the camp with the pairs of binoculars in his hand, meeting some of the other guests. He noticed the small red logo on the side of one of the two. He remembered that the game supervisor he had met on a previous trip had carried a pair of binoculars with just such a logo. Surely, if they were good enough for the top man at the safari lodge, then he would not look stupid using the same brand. This clinched the deal, even if the one with the red logo was 30 per cent more expensive. But he reassured himself 'that must be because of the great German lenses.' The power of a brand and its logo.

Corollary 3: Brand value is not necessarily determined by the message the company sends, rather by what the audience agrees it is.

How brands create utilitarian value

Jack explored the idea of what his buying experience could teach him about the function of the brand. He identified three sources of brand value for the end customer:

1. Efficiency: The three brands he had picked out had saved him time. They had convinced him that the quality was good, without having to spend time reading a lot of reviews or testing them out in the store. The brand had facilitated efficient selection.
2. Engagement: Two of the brands had strengthened his good safari mood as he associated them with travel and adventure. The brands had given him good emotions by association.
3. Belonging: The brand he finally selected helped him to strengthen his perceived position within his safari peer group. Its value was based on the assurance that he would stand out well in this audience. The brand communicated to others that he was the kind of guy who could afford the best possible equipment for his trip.

He made another sketch in his notebook. Het placed the three sources of brand value he had just identified in a pyramid:

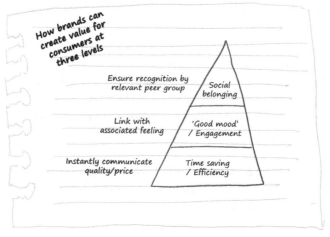

Figure 1.4: Three levels of brand value creation for end customers.

He checked how M&S was doing with respect to the three levels of the model he had sketched:
- Campaigns had been very effective in communicating the functional qualities of products. This is the comfort zone for M&S, no surprises there.
- Even though the quality of the advertisements created a recognizable association, it was now clear to Jack that the message was not fully trusted, as it did not align with the company's image.
- The social belonging aspect had been less obvious to Jack. Despite being deeply immersed in the use social apps to keep up with his extensive network; and despite peer perception being his key reason for choosing the binoculars with the red label, he had completely missed the importance of this value driver for M&S.

He turned, again, to the thorn in M&S's side, SunnyFountain. They seemed to be much more skewed toward the top of the pyramid.

- SunnyFountain had skipped the complex and sometimes boring process of selecting a product by skipping it altogether. It focused entirely on the next two levels of the pyramid
- By sharing fun stories on their culture, SunnyFountain had created a buzz that was shared between end customers, loading the brand with very positive associations.
- By creating an attractive, partly imaginary, peer group that people craved to join, end customers, who had witnessed the many discussions about the brand online, could be reasonably sure that a choice for SunnyFountain would be perceived positively by their peers.

Jack realized that M&S needed to step up its game, address the social belonging aspect of their brand pyramid, and push back against SunnyFountain. 'How can we beat this upstart at its own game? How can we leverage what we are, interact with our large customer base, and expand the role that the M&S brand plays in their interactions?'

As he put away his notebook, his attention returned to the impressive bovines. The guide started the engine, and they had an uneventful drive back to camp. After a large breakfast, they retired to the terrace in front of their tent, a shaded, comfortable spot, to do some leisurely work during the heat of the day.

Diversity in the Herd: Inhomogeneity in the customer base creates opportunity

Before he could fully dive into his laptop, he was distracted by the arrival of a four-wheel drive. They had planned a long game drive, all the way to the Mara River, where the large migrating herds were starting to pour onto the Masai Mara plains. They drove for over an hour across the savannah, only seeing the occasional topi antelope, standing  with its front legs on a termite mound looking out for predators.

As they approached the river, the landscape changed, the terrain became bushier. Despite the vegetation, they could spot the herds from a long distance. It looked like a swarm of bees, or a flock of birds, covering both sides of the river ravine.

As they got closer, Jack was more easily able to distinguish different species. Close by were the zebra, the rough mowing machines at the front of the herd. They arrived first to find a laid table of fresh, long grass. They were snapping up large volumes of easily accessible grass, moving on to stay ahead of the second wave, that of the wildebeest. The wildebeest are the core of the herd, by far the largest group. They would eat the nutritious leaves and ruminate them to get maximum food extraction. The size of the herds was clear evidence that this was an effective strategy. At the back of the migration, still on the other side of the river, came the small Thomson gazelles, the nibblers, who eat the small nutritious buds and new leaves that grow after the passing of the first two waves of the herd.

Jack concluded that segmentation in nature is much clearer than in business. There are easily distinguishable species, each with its own niche.

As they drove closer to the riverbank, they ended up standing in the middle of a never-ending flow of wildebeests pouring along either side of the car. Most the herd consisted of females with young that were born earlier that year in the fertile plains next to the

Ngoro-Ngoro crater. There were also juveniles embarking on their first solo trek. Then, there were the males, slightly larger.

As they watched for an hour or so, Jack noticed an increasing level of detail. This was a familiar effect; the longer you look, the more you see. The greater detail affords understanding at an entirely different level than you get from a short glance. This was the essence of going to the work floor *gemba*, the place where value is created. *Gemba* is part of the continuous improvement methodology that was at the base of Japanese manufacturing success in the '80s, and which was now widely copied, including by M&S.

For Jack, it now applied to the herd, the amorphous flow of similar wildebeests slowly became much less chaotic, and more transparent.

Some animals appeared to have a very light pattern of stripes. Some animals were slightly larger, some animals sped toward the open plain, others lingered longer on the edges of the bush aligned with the river. Some animals (usually the slightly larger ones) ventured into new patches of grass and ate their fill, at the risk of being ambushed in unfamiliar surroundings. Others were happy to focus on the more intensely grazed areas in the middle of the herd, having more difficulty filling their stomachs, but very safe from predators.

Jack was surprised at this variety. It was amazing to realize that this microdiversity was supported by the same landscape. Even as selective pressure constantly weeded out those animals that were less fit, the herd did not become homogeneous. Small variations in weather, vegetation, landscape, predators, luck, and competition must have created opportunities for the differences to survive. The diversity of the herd made it able to exploit many types of situations, thus reducing competition.

Corollary 4: Herds with higher levels of variety make them better able to appropriate resources in a varying set of microenvironments

As a baby boomer he felt more association with the large herd than with the niche species. 'I suppose that is because I have been born and bred in a family company that is clearly not a niche player,' he imagined. This started a train of thought back to the issue of the afternoon, whom should M&S target? Was their target group too wide compared to the focused approach of small, nimble competitors? Or could he learn something from the resilience of the large herd?

By the time they arrived back at the camp, it was getting dark. After a shower, they gathered for drinks and dinner. After dinner, he returned to his spot near the tent and opened his laptop.

How can M&S leverage the breadth of its customer base to create niche pockets of brand value?

Jack returned to his thoughts of the safari that day. He pondered how M&S could respond to SunnyFountain. What was the best way to counter this upstart startup stealing their game? How could M&S be outsmarted in the market, despite having a customer base that is at least 200 times larger, and an advertising budget at least ten times higher than SunnyFountain?

He summarized some key thoughts of the day:
– The more transparent M&S becomes, the more the trust in its message will increase
– M&S must deepen its interaction with its end customers, not just send messages
– M&S has a large end customer base. As you look closer the diversity increases.

Then, he expanded upon these thoughts.

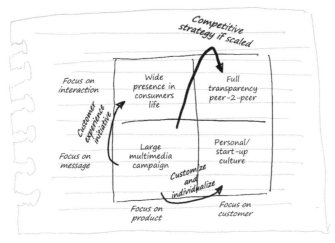

Figure 1.5: Large companies should leverage their customer base peer-to-peer and create trust through transparency.

- Copying the startup culture would not be feasible for a company the size of M&S. It would reduce the difference and make it easier for SunnyFountain to beat them from their core advantage, they were a startup!
- M&S has a much larger end customer base but it is not exploiting its potential. The first step, surely, would be to improve the experience that this huge customer base has when interacting with M&S. This would be a powerful response to SunnyFountain.
- The large end customer base could bring an even more valuable competitive advantage if they could be connected emotionally to the brand, through the values at the heart of M&S.

He decided that his best option was to beat SunnyFountain at social engagement by leveraging their large existing customer base.

Jack drew alternatives for M&S to move away from the multichannel push approach.

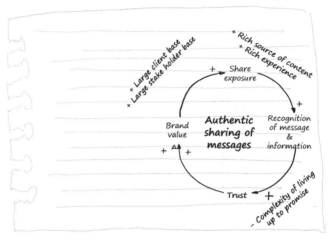

Figure 1.6: A large customer base is a huge bridgehead in conquering social brand value.

It occurred to him that the one thing holding back large firms is their inability to live up to their promise to be fully transparent. He was convinced that at the root of this problem is lackluster, process-oriented management of a company, i.e. a lack of leadership at the top and an inability to execute transparency down through the ranks. 'Surely this was not going to be an issue in his family's firm?' However, it dawned on him that even M&S had to overhaul the way they were accustomed to interacting with their end customers. But how should they engage with such a large and diverse end customer base?

He returned to his line of thought:

– To create trust in its marcom messages M&S needs to be transparent about how it lives it values in the company and the way it produces.
– M&S should create social brand value for the audience by leveraging its large end customer base.

Social brand value means that people are going to talk about M&S. 'How realistic is this? Would end customers actually engage in these kinds of online activities?' 'How could he expect the average end customer of M&S to write engaging content online?'

The complexity of the customer base adds a further complication to building the social brand value. Just like the herds of wildebeest, the closer you look, the bigger the variety you observe. The customer base does not consist of homogenous segments, but of many stakeholders with great individual differences. M&S's prominent position in the market means that it is supplying many different product models to many different users: Professionals, amateurs, families, outdoor folk, regular users, biannual users. Within these groups there is a difference in interest, in preferred channels, in the role of the M&S brand, in the peer group, ... the list goes on.

There must be hundreds of places where the end customers could meet each other online, but Jack realized that many of these groups would rarely cross paths frequently. He needed to let go of the paradigm that he should focus on concentrated, highly visible social media heroes to spread the message. This would never work with such a large and diverse group.

Instead, he needed to use the diversity of his client base to make specific relevant content for each of the many micro niches that constitute the mass of buyers. The release of such an enormous amount of specific content would have two advantages for M&S:
– As the incumbent market leader, M&S is in a better position that any startup to cast a wide net of information to address a much more diversified audience. A substantial part of the budget could be freed up for this without the need to push above the line.
– Because of the broad set of end customers, M&S could leverage a much wider, more diversified community to engage with, again something that would pose a huge challenge for new entrants.

He redrew his circle diagram of how open sharing of messages in a connected world could reinforce trust. He then added the pros and cons of a large incumbent.

The conclusion was staring him in the face. If M&S can live up to its promises and become more transparent, the potential, as an incumbent, for its products to dominate online presence is huge. The arrival of peer-to-peer that he had seen as a threat was now a huge opportunity to strengthen its position. By engaging with the client base and accepting less control over the message, M&S could steer itself toward a trusted partner at the heart of the industry.

Corollary 5: An incumbent's large community of customers is a great source of competitive advantage if leveraged to create brand value.

This brought Jack to the next challenge: How to execute all of this? How to support this content with a genuine culture of transparency? How to make sure that what is communicated to the outside, is in line with what was happening on the inside. The fact that it is hard to achieve means that there must be some handicap in it that can be exploited to create trustworthiness. He felt he could make a difference in line with the heritage of his family's business. As the evening drew to a close, he wrote a reply to Nancy:

From: Jack
To: Nancy

Subject: Marketing & brand building in the digital age

Hi Nancy,

Thank you for your exhaustive analysis of the recent campaign efforts, even if the news is not good. My trip to Africa has given me the opportunity to take a step back. I have come to the conclusion that we need to make some profound changes in the way we approach branding and marketing communications to remain effective. Here is why:

– Our end customers have increased access to information and to exchange with other customers; consequently, we cannot rely solely on the size of our campaign to convince them of our brand qualities.

– Increasing investment in a message that is not recognized in our company's behavior will increase the discrepancy between the message and how customers perceive it. It is counterproductive, as it reduces trust.

– Brands must be transparent across all aspects of the business to which customers relate. This effectively transfers a message that is falsifiable by customers and will therefore be seen as unreliable.

– Our internal culture must align with the message we send out to the world. This will be our biggest challenge, as it quite different from how we currently work.

– We need to develop this message jointly with our end customer community.

– The size and diversity of our customer community is the real competitive advantage we can leverage vis-à-vis these new but growing threats.

The consequence for our branding and marcom strategies are profound. We need to focus our attention on four action points:

- Orchestrate all end customers interaction with the brand and the product: Public, Direct, Product (CRM, social media moderation, content, above the line, service)
- Ensure a consistent end-to-end experience in order not to lose the trust of our end customers.
- Create specific recognition among smaller niches, vegetarians, trackers, families, parties, etc.
- Leverage existing client contacts, distribution contacts, as well as other communities: homeowners, customer organizations, whisky brands, meat, producers, organic chains, etc.

I would like to discuss the impact of this analysis at our next Marcom team meeting. To maximize our speed of execution on what emerges from this meeting I would like you to prepare the following points, please:

- Prepare an analysis of how our internal culture, habits, and values compare to our external messages, where they are in line, where they are different.
- Please sit down with Tom from operations to identify the top-10 discrepancies. Then asses our ability to address them, even if it takes a considerable reset in the way we source.
- With your team suggest 10 very specific target segments that we could engage to start a conversation. They need to have a common passion about the use of our product.
- In line with your suggestion, please put the investment in the current campaign on hold. Ask our agency to come up with a plan for supporting a more diversified interactive conversation with our end customers.

I hope you get the gist of where I am going. Let's spend some time when I get back running through these ideas more extensively.

Regards,

Jack

Introduction Chapter 2: Trouble in the sales channels, leading distributor threatens to leave

As he wrapped up for the night, he took a last glance at his mailbox. Just when he thought he had cut this Gordian knot on marketing, he was presented with a new issue, this time in sales. Dan Hirscht had forwarded a mail on a conflict about ecommerce with OutdoorKings, an important distributor. The distributor was threatening to withdraw M&S products from their portfolio if M&S continued its aggressive direct online approach. Jack decided he was going to leave this question for tomorrow, instead he poured two glasses of whisky and sat down with Caroline to enjoy the sounds of the African night.

2. Channel conflict: Building rich revenue through value adding channels

Browsing antelopes – Uncertainty, distance, and richness of experience drive the switch between resources

The next morning, Jack woke up while it was still dark, as the morning coffee was brought to the tent, in time for a game drive at sunrise. Jack loved this time of day in Africa. The sounds were still of the night, dominated by frogs, hippos, hyenas, and lions. In half an hour, it would suddenly quieten down. After a short interval of silence, a first bird would call, and soon the birds would dominate the noises around the camp.

As they stepped into the four-wheel drive, he pondered the question that had touched him last night, how should he handle the discussion about sales channel conflicts?

That morning, they decided to park close to a waterhole to see if any game arrived for a drink. Jack was sitting on the side looking away from the hole, gazing across the savannah. The area had a light distribution of bushes, close to a dry river. He saw a herd of impala moving from one group of bushes to the next, browsing their way toward the vehicle.

As the herd came closer, Jack noticed how the impala moved intermittently. They would eat a group of shrubs together, until the juiciest bits had gone, and then move to the next set of shrubs. 'How did they decide when to move?' Jack recalled an online lecture he had viewed some time ago.

Choosing from two options whilst browsing might seem like a mundane task, but for these animals it is a life-or-death balance, between dying from a lack of food or getting killed by moving in open grassland terrain. The animal with the best strategy would produce the most offspring. Ultimately, those who chose the right behavior would become dominant.

It was no surprise to Jack, an ardent naturalist, that this behavior is highly optimized. There was even some clever math to prove it, the Marginal Value theorem. He sketched the figure in his notepad.

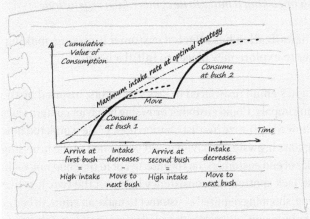

Figure 2.1: The Marginal Value theorem shows that browsers can acquire more food by optimizing the timing of their switch to the next bush.

Jack considered what conditions might affect the best strategy.
- Larger shrubs meant that it would take longer before the food became diminished.
- Higher quality browsing would mean that it would take longer for the food to diminish.
- The longer the distance to next shrub, the more it makes sense to stay put longer.
- Uncertainty about what to expect at the next shrub, equates to a greater distance, and would lead to a longer stay.

There are social factors, too:
- Synchronizing movement with the herd reduces the risk of being ambushed by a predator.
- A weaker or smaller animal needs to move earlier, as the larger, stronger animals would claim the remaining food at a shrub.

Slowly, the impala moved beyond the vehicle to the other side, out of Jack's sight. There was still not much moving at the waterhole. Jack's deliberations drifted to other subjects.

> *Corollary 6: Antelope, such as impalas, browsing for food, face the choice of continuing to graze on a diminishing bush or risking a move to new, more lush vegetation.*

How digitalization has affected customer browsing, making it easier to explore new places to fulfill a need

Last night's email resurfaced in Jack's thoughts, inspired by the browsing impala. Could customer browsing behavior contain clues about how to optimize his distribution policy? He wondered how the impala's browsing behavior could be applied to the browsing behavior of end customers, on the internet or in the shopping mall.

First, Jack spotted the consistency between the two. Just like browsing, shopping required a customer to make an effort, to better their life, by acquiring a particular good or service. Even if shopping is not a life-or-death situation, the same mechanism applies to both customer shopping and impala browsing. (He noticed that some people, including his teenage daughter might disagree. They would say that shopping the right look could be a life-or-death experience).

> *Corollary 7: Customers, just like browsing impalas, continuously must make choices about whether to stay or move on when fulfilling a need, such as choosing between different e-commerce sites, retail outlets, established brands, and new brands.*

Jack zoomed in his thinking on some of the parallels with the impalas

— At any point, a customer can decide to acquire what is in front of him/her, and what is familiar, or decide to search further.

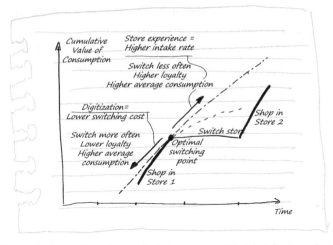

Figure 2.2: Marginal Value theorem for browsers suggest that digitalization reduces customer loyalty due to lower switching costs

- If the current provider has a wider assortment, a customer can stay longer at that provider, without considering a change.
- If it takes more effort to switch, e.g. the distance to the next shop is greater, or the amount of searching online takes more effort, the cost will increase, making it more beneficial to stick with the current provider.
- If the switch involves a new or unknown product, brand, or outlet, the perceived cost will increase, making it more beneficial to stay with the current provider.

Jack now considered how the growth of digital was changing retail dynamics. The next shop is only a button away, thus the effort of switching is reduced. It also gives greater insight for comparison and an ability to predict the quality of a new product, making it less risky to switch to a new source. The reduced switching costs affect loyalty to brands or providers.

Furthermore, instead of everyone simultaneously watching a commercial during a dedicated time slot in the evening, and then going to the shop the next morning to purchase it, digital channels provide information and access to buying opportunities wherever and whenever the customer wants.

Digital commerce has the same effect on customer browsing as shortening the distance between shrubs for impala.

The impact of social media on purchase decisions is increasingly evident. By communicating with a wide peer group, customers are better able to manage the social risks of a purchase.

On the other hand, Jack also realized that digital media could lead to overkill, i.e. that increased amounts of information and offers would increasingly confuse the customer. There is a role for a limited set of editors/guides/pathfinders to filter the information in order to maintain the overview. This role can be played by a social group, a blogger, or a forum, but is done even more efficiently by a brand or a provider.

Corollary 8: The rise of digitalization has changed the way customers browse and make decisions about products and services. Reduced switching costs make it easier for customers to change brands. However, it has also increased the risk of making a poor choice due to the abundance of information and options available.

Jack realized how his branding analysis from the previous day fitted neatly into this conclusion. An abundance of information reduces the effectiveness of old school marketing communication.

He further explored the role of a retailer in the life of a customer when acquiring a product. Customers go to retailers to acquire products or services that will improve some aspect of their life, but there is some effort (browsing) involved. This not only involves the money a customer spends, but also the time and effort, as well as the unpleasant exposure to the uncertainty of not knowing whether the effort will lead them to the right product. How can a retailer ensure that a customer will browse at its branches? Jack made a list of three ways a retailer can add value in the optimization of acquisition:

1. Efficiency: Ensure that the customer minimizes the effort invested in the acquisition. This might entail minimizing travel time, searching time, time lost on comparing products. Risk can also be perceived as effort, so minimizing the risk of buying the wrong product increases efficiency.
2. Effectiveness: The ultimate acquisition is one that does exactly the job you need it to do, functionally, emotionally, and socially. To increase effectiveness, retailers must provide alternatives, widen and deepen their assortment, and offer information that helps customers to assess what is available and, of course, for the best price!
3. Engagement: Not all shopping is seen as effort; some might even see it as a treat. For some purchases, the shopping experience may create value. By ensuring that the experience is as positive as possible, retailers can shift both the efficiency balance and the effectiveness balance their way. This is especially powerful if the shopping experience becomes a social one, i.e. not a family with crying children, but a group of friends jointly acquiring stuff that meets the group's approval.

Jack drew a small sketch of his version of the three-level pyramid model:

Customer will constantly try to optimize in the first two stages of the pyramid, effectiveness and efficiency. This is where the impact of e-commerce is most felt, and this is the focus of many fights between producers and retailers, i.e. reducing cost to become the most effective solution for the customer as efficiency advantages are lost due to digitalization.

Efficiency might be crucial when it comes to attracting a customer to the local supermarket for the weekly groceries. For a large ticket item, however, the customer will invest more effort to optimize the value or suitability of the acquisition.

Engagement, at the top of the pyramid, adds a dimension that is not so directly affected by ecommerce. If the shopping trip is

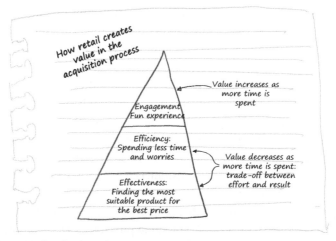

Figure 2.3: Three levels at which retail creates value for customers.

just for fun. For example, buying clothes with friends, spending more time can lead to increased value. Some might argue that true social shopping is a similar alternative, but the impact is still limited.

Different customers might end up in different modes for the same category. For example, to some, cooking is a value-adding experience; others just want to eat something to fill their stomachs.

The same customer might end up in different modes over time. For example, a customer might usually order a pizza. but for a dinner party with friends the same person will cook a great meal.

Social belonging, at the top of the branding pyramid that Jack had explored the day before, adds another dimension. If a current provider is accepted by the customer's peer group but a new candidate is not, the risk to switching increases, as the message sent with the new brand might not be right. On the other hand, if all the popular people are switching to the new brand, it is socially risky to stay with the old one.

Corollary 9: Engagement and social belonging are sources of value that are much less affected by the impact of ecommerce, unlike the value of efficiency and effectiveness in the acquisition process.

Excursion to Narok village: Retail trends toward a level playing field

After breakfast, back at the camp, Jack and Caroline walked to the reception. They hopped into a minivan to the nearby town of Narok to buy some batteries for their torch, as well as to have a look around.

Narok is a typical, small African town with one asphalt road, leading to a collection of houses, which slowly change from clay to concrete as you get closer to the center. In the town center, a busy market/bus station/parking lot is dotted with small stalls, mostly selling one type of fruit or vegetable. On the side, are some small convenience stores (calling themselves supermarkets).

Jack felt like he had stepped back into historic retailing. Most merchandise consisted of local produce, offered by private individuals, small allotment holders, who would sell peer-to-peer, one familiar face to another. It was harder for a customer to evaluate the quality of non-local items (including batteries), and they were very expensive. Jack had trouble finding the right batteries. Compared to this problem, the abundance of goods in large American malls looked much more favorable.

He entered a small store, where he picked up a package of suitable batteries. It was not priced, so he held it up to the seller behind the counter: 'Can you tell me the price of these?' One pack was 7000 Ksh (Kenyan Shillings), about €7, probably twice the price it would cost at home. He expressed his surprise about the high price to the seller, who gave him a big smile and signaled for him to come closer to the counter. The seller picked up his phone. He opened an e-commerce site for a store in Nairobi, which showed a price that was only slightly lower. Jack was taken aback: in all his shopping experiences, he had never encountered a salesperson who opened the internet to compare prices. Even an US retailer could learn from this service level.

Jack felt happier; knowing that he was not being ripped off, but that this was just the going price of batteries in Kenya. He evens added some more batteries as well as a nice compact flashlight, as a spare. As he walked out, he saw a sign on the store that surprised him: 'We deliver your shopping free of charge'. The sign looked like the ones in the store where his grandma would take him in his childhood, forty years ago. 'Please order by phone' had been added with a marker. 'Amazon Prime in Narok!' What a surprise. 'I guess the low cost of wages allows for this kind of service level'. In the US, the productivity level would be much too low to do this sustainably, although rising wage inequality did open some avenues for building such services, even if he felt this was not desirable.

He decided that in his further analysis of the distribution question, he would not limit himself to planning only e-commerce and shops, but would expand his thinking, aware that retail had always had large variety of service models.

How the low switching costs of e-commerce reduce the ability of retailers to claim position with a customer

Jack's thoughts returned to this morning's email and the angry threats from OutdoorKings. He had met Frank Smorssens, the CEO of OutdoorKings, some years ago over lunch. Frank had used a napkin to explain his view of his retail business.

In any one region, he builds a network of outlets, in high-traffic locations, filled with a new category of assortment of substantial size. He then claims this product category so aggressively, through choice and price, that any competitor considering entering the region would struggle to make a profit in that category. By expanding the network, he reaps the benefits of scale. It provides enough volume to invest in mass marketing further reducing the chance for a competitor to build up competing outlets in the selected region. Frank had drawn a circle that showed a self-enhancing profit model. He concluded by smiling and saying, 'you see, that is why we are so crucial for the success of your company in this segment, and that is why I have to insist on improving the price conditions of your offer.'

Clearly, Frank was not smiling anymore! If you could compare prices of batteries online in Narok, then the invasion of alternative

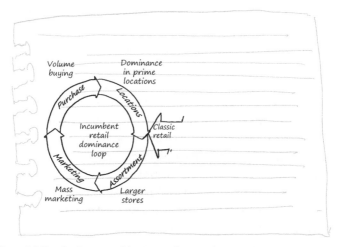

Figure 2.4: The classic source of dominance for incumbent retailers is based on their scale: dominance in locations, media, and buying volume

sales channels in Chicago or Denver would be inevitable. Jack considered how technology trends reduced barriers to entry further:

- It is simple to start a web shop and instantly, (via UPS or others) reach the whole of the US, avoiding the rent costs paid by OutdoorKings.
- It would be easier to stock a substantial assortment or get a part of it financed by the producer.
- Instead of expensive above-the-line marketing campaigns, scalable pay-as-you-use search items are available to generate traffic.

'So this is all great thinking,' Jack pondered as he stepped back into the minivan, 'but I do not believe retail stores will disappear. It does not really help me to solve the dilemma posed by Dan Hirscht.'

Caroline entered the van with a beautiful ceramic vase she had acquired. Initially, she had been reluctant to shop, but there was a very convincing young local who had spent ten minutes joking with her, talking her into at least taking a look at the vases. She

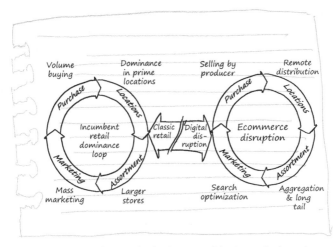

Figure 2.5: E-commerce disrupts the classic source of dominance for incumbent retailers.

had paid €65, probably a multiple of the normal price, but she was quite happy, as she had really enjoyed the experience with the local souvenir stall, staffed by family of the local artist that had made the vase.

Back at the lodge, lunch was served. As soon as they could leave the buffet, he and Caroline moved to the tent. Jack reflected on his insights from the game drive and the visit to Narok.

The ideal shop is one with great choice, easy selection, instant availability, a great experience, and the lowest price. It provides the highest value as it ensures the most effective fulfilment of a need with the least effort whilst having fun. Each aspect of this proposition cost a retailer money. A retailer keen to maximize price without losing the customer to a competitor.

By blocking competitive outlets, OutdoorKings was trying to ensure that switching to another shop would entail driving to another town, a big effort that greatly reduces customer efficiency. Consequently, OutdoorKings can afford to provide a less effective proposition, for instance by raising prices.

Jack now understood why OutdoorKings was so upset about the arrival of e-commerce.

As he looked up and stared over the grassland next to the camp, Jack's thoughts on e-commerce started to become clearer. 'It's about the way retailers and customer interact, and how e-commerce disrupts this balance'.

This disruption increases price transparency and reduces differentiation. At the low end of the price spectrum, dominated by powerful retailers, this disruption can lead to an online price war, sucking the profitability of whole categories, such as TVs and PCs, down the drain.

Some producers have sought to protect their brands from this onslaught from commodity magnets by making their products and distribution more exclusive. This approach reduces the role of retailers and pushes producers into the position of niche players. M&S was to broadly spread to move its assortment to an exclusive niche.

Corollary 10: E-commerce puts a cap on the ability of retailers to exploit local physical domination.

This insight only strengthened the importance of the conundrum with the company's distributor. How should M&S manage its role as producer vs retailer in such way that the category remains healthy?

The Giraffe vs Acacia – Competing parties in the value chain need each other for survival

The light in the camp began to change as Mike arrived to take them on the evening game drive. They moved through the savannah with a stunning view of acacia trees and gently sloping hills in the background. They did not encounter too many animals. When they spotted a group of giraffes, they decided to stop to observe them strolling among the trees, browsing, in the rich light that was slowly turning golden as the sun started to set.

As Jack gazed over the savannah, he observed that all the trees had an umbrella shape. They were completely bare of leaves under the umbrella. All the umbrellas were of the same height, just high enough for the giraffes to reach the lowest leaves with their long tongues. An equilibrium had materialized between the height of the giraffe and the height of the trees. A daily tug of war had arisen between giraffe and acacia.

He decided that evolution was great, but not perfect. If the trees and the giraffes jointly decided to be one meter less tall, nothing would change in the equilibrium, but both the giraffe and the trees would save a lot of energy.

Conversely, he wondered why the trees did not grow higher. It would take less than a meter for them to be completely out of reach. The giraffes would only be able to browse the smaller trees that did not invest in the extra height. Why did this not happen? What mechanism was keeping the acacias at their current height; the height at which the giraffe can just reach the lowest levels?

If the trees grow taller, of course the giraffes could grow taller as well, but at some stage this would not be sustainable for the giraffes. It would disappear or change its choice of foliage, probably losing its height forever.

At that point, lower trees or bushes would have a big advantage over the acacia, as they could expend their energy on growing leaves and seeds, rather than stem and height.

Jack concluded that rejecting the current height equilibrium would ultimately be a losing strategy for a tree.

The giraffes were probably optimizing their height in the same way. Becoming smaller would lead to starvation. Becoming taller would become a competitive disadvantage that the extra access to foliage did not make up for.

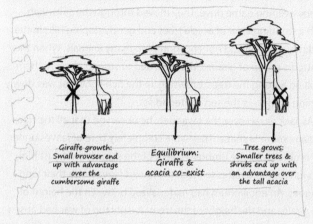

Figure 2.6: Giraffes and acacia trees have established a height equilibrium.

Jack was no mathematician, but after seeing the film *A Beautiful Mind* he had read up on Game Theory and this seemed to be a Nash Equilibrium to him.

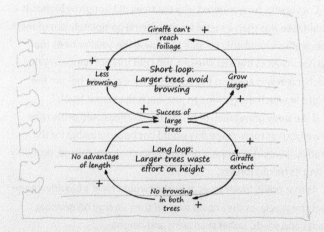

Figure 2.7: In the game between the giraffe and the acacia, a taller tree would get less browsing in the short term, but lose out to smaller trees once giraffes are extinct.

If some conditions change, such as the fertility of the soil or amount of rainfall, the giraffe and acacia game would probably result in a slightly different equilibrium. That is nature's way of responding to change. If the balance shifts, it finds a new stable position.

It now dawned on Jack that this was a perfect paradigm for approaching his e-commerce dilemma, which had been floating in the back of his head all day.

How optimal distribution strategy focuses on the value it creates for the customer, instead of share or revenue

Jack and Caroline had drinks at their tent. As Caroline drifted away in the pages of a movie script she was editing, Jack opened his laptop in order not to lose the ideas from the evening trip.

The dilemma facing OutdoorKings was not new. Producers and retailers have always been in a game of optimization, seeking a balance, just like the giraffe and the acacia. 'If I get a clearer understanding of this balance, it will help me to make the right choices at M&S in the conflicts with our distributor.' In the same way that giraffes and acacia trees can coexist peacefully and avoid the struggle for dominance that will leave both at a disadvantage.

When producers go direct, they lose mass distribution, and their brand tends to transform into a niche brand. When retailers use brands to fight for price leadership, either a low-cost dollar store or the online marketplace will end up with a large chunk of the volume. In both cases, much of the value of a category will be lost.

Jack could find five models for competition and sorted them, from poor to rich. It illustrated to him how a proposition shifts toward a rich proposition that allows the category to claim a larger share of wallet from the customer market.

1. **Price.** Cost can be dramatically reduced by sharply reducing assortment and service. So much so that a customer is willing to sacrifice some efficiency and choice. This is the model adopted by dollar stores or outdoor town markets.

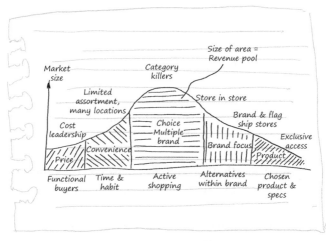

Figure 2.8: Rich retail propositions combine decent margins with substantial volume.

2. **Convenience.** By expanding network, opening hours, and speed of service, customers can get quick and easy access to fulfill any ad hoc or even urgent needs. This is the model adopted by some pharmacy chains, convenience stores, and McDonalds.

3. **Choice** By expanding choice whilst ensuring a reasonable level of pricing, customers get an extremely efficient and effective acquisition solution, for which they are willing to pay slightly more. This is the model of the Mall, Amazon, but also of regular shopping such as groceries.

4. **Experience** By improving the experience, customers are less penalized, or even rewarded for spending more time browsing or searching. This allows for higher prices and less effective solutions. This is the model of the boutique shopping street or merchandise stores in theme parks.

5. **Exclusivity** The most attractive model for the value chain is to have unique products that are coveted by customers. This is where shops owned by producers do add value, as inefficiency in acquisition is perceived as valuable. Examples include Apple and Louis Vuitton.

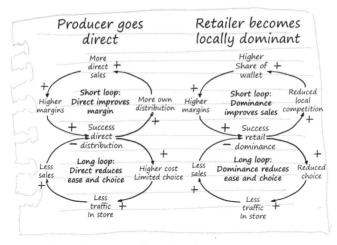

Figure 2.9: The game between retailers and producers suggests that a mutual balance creates the 'richest' pool of revenue.

If retailers and producers can shift many customers in a category toward a 'rich' proposition, their category will do well, and will attract good margin revenue. If not, the whole system of trade and producers will end up in a price war, and the profitable euros will end up in another category.

Jack concluded: 'Dominance of the retailer or the producer both deteriorates the 'richness' of the customer experience'.

'We must prevent this race to the bottom at all costs in our category,' Jack whispered to himself. He thought of examples where this shift had gone in the wrong direction, such as books, consumer electronics, and white goods. He also realized that there are examples of value chains successfully addressing the trend, such as the Apple ecosystem, the ecological food category, and luxury goods.

Jack pondered: 'Where does an acacia /giraffe ecosystem survive?' 'What drives reinforcement of this interaction, and what drives instability and replacement by other systems?' Earlier, Jack had described the system as a game between giraffe and tree, and that the savannah that morning was in an equilibrium, i.e.

moving away from the balance, either higher or lower, would be detrimental to both giraffe and tree.

Jack realized in that in the natural environment, the equilibrium could always be broken by change. If the cost of moving from the equilibrium becomes lower, a small distortion could mean the system becomes unstable and the combination would be lost. Only when the cost of moving away from the equilibrium is high is the equilibrium likely to be sustained for some time. The change is that the giraffe/acacia system only appears in areas where the equilibrium is stable due to the high costs of moving.

To find out what sustains the giraffe/acacia ecosystem, one must understand what could strengthen the equilibrium, i.e. what could raise the cost of diverting away from the equilibrium?

- In areas with abundant rain and nutrients, the trees would easily be able to grow higher with little punishment. Jack surmised that he would hardly ever see acacias next to rivers with more fertile sediments. Instead, shrubs, or the beautiful yellow-barked fever trees would be dominant.
- In areas where there are no alternative food sources for giraffes, the species would disappear faster as soon as there was any increase in average height. There would be no alternatives to keep the giraffes alive.

Jack could think of some characteristics that would affect the stability of the equilibrium.

- If giraffes can switch between areas, they might simply live elsewhere and occasionally visit the area, rebalancing the old equilibrium
- The lack of giraffe browsing could be offset by trees growing bigger and attracting other herbivores, such as elephants.

It was clear to Jack that for M&S to influence the quality of the retail ecosystem, they would need to work together with the retailer to manage the characteristics of the business they are in. He should focus on rigging the system such that the penalty of either a retailer or a producer moving up or down the price ladder would be maximized.

He wrote down some characteristics that could ensure that the ecosystem would stay healthy, and some that might lead to a price war or a niche market.

- What would increase the penalty on a retailer for replacing the producer's brand with its own?
  - alternative sales channels for the producer might steer away traffic
  - lack of availability of decent own brand producers might increase the cost of creating an own brand
  - differentiation in existing products, making it more expensive to create an attractive alternative
  - lower pricing might not fully be compensated by lower sourcing costs
- What would increase the penalty on a producer for going down in the value line, for instance by starting a price war with a low-quality product?
  - Availability of retailers brand at lower price would reduce volume or jeopardizing the producer's existing high margins
  - extensive choice of the product in retail would increase the cost of creating a more attractive own channel alternative

For M&S, the current position of dominance it shares with retail partners is worth saving. Jack checked how he could skew the category dynamics to make it more stable.

The key to blocking the industry moving down the price ladder is to ensure that no alternative party can profitably build up a low-cost alternative:

- Further improvements in M&S production would need to ensure that they remain cost leader, especially at the lower-end volume market.

- Jack decided to produce for some of the big box retailers that he had always kept outside the door in order to protect the brand. He would now sell them a basic version of the products.
- He would expand e-commerce, as an alternative, but not as an objective in itself. He would ensure a dealer finder, to encourage users to mix a physical channel into the total buying experience.

To avoid the move to a niche product:

- Jack would cancel the flagship store project, and instead make the product range available to his key trading partners.
- He would expand in-store support for selected retailers.
- He would bring the distribution channel into the total experience, to make a more diverse and differentiated offer based on the same single technical product. He would make this available to his trading partners.

This approach could be well-supported by the professional products arm of his business. Even if this customer group is small, the professional use of his products, and the entrepreneurship of his professional customers is a great asset to the brand.

> *Corollary 11: Producers and sales channels should strive for a balance that creates a rich category. Partners should structure their commercial system in order to increase the stability of this equilibrium.*

Finally, Jack decided that the direction of the marcom investment, toward direct engagement, provided a great opportunity to manage the channel. If they were able to create a direct link with potential buyers, then they could facilitate digital buyers purchasing direct and engaged buyers visiting a retail channel. A highly engaged audience would best be served with a brick-and-mortar service proposition, with skilled advisors, good selection, back-up warranty, and service.

From: Jack
To: Dan

Subject: Redefining our cooperation with distribution partners

Hi Dan,

Thank you for your heads up on the conflict that seems to be brewing with one of our key distributors. I believe we should continue to intensify our direct relationship with end customers via digital channels, but at the same time work closely together with OutdoorKings. Here is why:

— Our end customers have the choice to spend their money on many thousands of alternative categories. We are just one of these alternatives. Together with our suppliers and distribution, which includes OutdoorKings, we compete with other categories for a share of the end customer's wallet.
— Our category will only attract rich end customers' euros if the product as well as the experience of buying, using, and sharing is more attractive than that of the next category.
— If we can build a collaborative and rich experience, together with our retail partners, over the lifecycle of the product, we will jointly attract more euros. If cooperation deteriorates, experience diminishes, and price will remain the only differentiator. Price comparison becomes dominant, and the distributors will face a price fight with the likes of Walmart, which has stocked a limited range of our core products for years.
— A strong category and a rich experience require well laid out retail outlets and highly qualified personnel, in convenient locations where our products can be acquired together with other relevant products. This remains the core of our channel strategy, as our brand stands for quality, not just of the product, but of the total experience, including choice, right selection, decent warranty, and great user experience.

– We will accelerate our investment in these sales channels, to ensure the quality of this experience: in sales training; in exclusive assortment for selected distributors; and in point-of-sale materials. We will seek higher-end customer price points for these products. We are happy to include OutdoorKings in this program.

– A strong category nowadays includes an online channel, as this is the preferred shopping method for some customers, and it is an important part of the journey for many others. Leaving the online channel open will lead to loss of revenue for the whole category and will open the door for less established players. Therefore, M&S cannot refrain from entering this channel.

– We will further develop the online channel, with a limited assortment, extensive information in cooperation with a few selected retail partners. We are happy to invite OutdoorKings to be the first partner to join this channel. OutdoorKings is a partner that is well-positioned to become a major enabler of a rich online retail experience, which must include many products that are outside our scope. We are happy to support OutdoorKings in achieving this position.

I would like to discuss the impact of this analysis at our next sales distribution meeting. To maximize our speed of execution on what emerges from this meeting, I would like you to prepare the following points, please:

– Cancel the flagship store project preparations; we need to invest this money in the traffic via our current distributors.
– Please sit down with Nancy from MarCom, to initiate two new projects:
  • Development of a 1-9 sq. meter point-of-sale concept, including training materials for store sales staff. They should focus on retail channel exclusives, such as the 'Barcelona' or 'Sevilla' range.

- *A concept to co-develop more local marketing initiatives, especially online or via social media, targeting end customers in local communities.*

Needless to say, both need to fit seamlessly into a single experience!

I hope you get the gist of where I am going with this. Let's spend some time when I get back running through these ideas more extensively.

Regards, Jack

Introduction Chapter 3: Innovation dilemma, the startup initiative is not gaining traction in the corporation.

As he pushed the send button, Jack realized that, by now, his team must have started wondering what kind of local tea he was drinking or herb he was smoking, for that matter. He was not too worried about causing confusion, however. His team was very qualified. The individual members would follow their own, sound judgment, following up on his ideas. He was excited about his newfound insights. He glanced through his mailbox to see if there was any other urgent business. A recent email from Daniel at business development caught his attention. Daniel was a young, technically gifted recruit, whom he had tasked with bringing digital innovation to the product range. Anticipating some resistance within the organization, he had set up a small, separate department, in a separate location, close to the university campus. As Jack did not know exactly what he was looking for, he had given Daniel and his team a relatively free hand. He had also committed some of his own time to directly supervising the team's progress and give coaching.

Jack suspected that Daniel reaching out to him was not a good sign. Sure enough, the email did much to wash away his bright mood. Daniel's team was spending a lot of time on developing a 'smart' version of their product for the home. Even if the exact nature of this product was still somewhat vague, Jack had decided to go for it, to engage with these new developments; after all, doing nothing was not an option. Now, the team was encountering an increasing number of setbacks on both the hardware and the software sides. After nine months, they had only produced a handful of small working prototypes, but each time the result had been killed off, as the new apps were not adding anything new to the rapidly developing market. Daniel now reported further setbacks. They had to expand the hardware to support more protocols, as the market demanded this from these kinds of devices. Additionally, the marketing team had rejected the latest app. It deemed the functionality neither attractive nor innovative enough for today's market.

Jack decided to put this to one side for the next day and walked over to the restaurant for a late dinner, followed by a presentation by a local research team on their work on bats in the Masai Mara.

3. Innovation in the crowd: Switching attention from startup to scaleup

Hyena vs vultures – Predictable revenue determines optimal operating model for innovation

The next morning they were awakened slightly earlier than normal. Mike the guide seemed quite excited as he had picked up the sound of a water buffalo being attacked by lions not too far from the camp.

After a quick gulp of coffee, they drove out into the chilly morning, anxious about the possibility of seeing a kill. Nowhere is the confrontation with nature more intense than in a lion kill. In one scene, both the dramatic beauty
of the savannah vividly combines with the savage and cruel fate of some animals. As many tourist vehicles cluster around such a scene when spotted, Jack felt a bit like a disaster tourist. This did not prevent him from being deeply touched by the scenes he observed. A tendency to explain what was happening in more favorable terms, such as the fact that animals needed to eat and that without these kills the grass would soon be overgrazed, had long eluded him, as he was zooming in on the essence of life and death being played out in front of his eyes in often slow, cruel scenes. He had often discussed these thoughts with Caroline. This was one of many things that united them in the way they experienced nature.

As they arrived on the scene, they witnessed a scene of utter mayhem. Six lions had grasped onto a young male buffalo on the side of the herd. They had mauled it so much that it was unable to move further. At the same time, the herd had turned on the lions to chase them away but could not stay with the wounded animal. It was a matter of time before they would move on. In the meantime, the lions were engaged in a back-and-forth with the herd.

Mike parked the Land Rover close to some other vehicles from the camp. They watched the scene unfold. Before long, the herd lost the urge to attack. They were chased off by the lions who now killed off the young buffalo. Soon, they were opening the animal, gorging themselves on the intestines. It was unusual for lions to hunt buffalo in times of abundant wildebeest, but the animal was probably already hurt or wounded, which had triggered the pride to go after it.

The morning chill was now quickly driven away by the sun. As the heat intensified, a steady flow of vultures began to arrive in a nearby  tree. Jack was amazed at the effectiveness of the vultures in spotting carrion. It was due to their excellent eyesight, but even more so, their clever behavior. In the morning, vultures wait for the first sun to create rising air currents. These currents allow them to the glide with minimum energy and spread out to cover a huge area, scanning the ground, but also watching each other. As soon as one vulture starts to descend, others will notice and follow. In this way, a ripple travels through the network of floating birds with some animals being pulled in from many kilometers away. Without any organization, vultures were cooperating very effectively.

By now, the lions had sated their appetites and moved away into the shade. As the vultures approached cautiously, the lions would get up and give chase once or twice, but they soon succumbed to leisurely resting and digesting the meal. Before long, the entire tree of birds had descended and was now one mass of clapping wings and snapping bills, each trying to grasp as much as possible before nothing was left but a clean skeleton.

The excitement had not gone unnoticed by some other scavengers. The ubiquitous striped jackal had snapped up some morsels in the mayhem. Just as the scene started to quieten down, some hyena appeared. They were wary, as lions do not look kindly upon them. They easily chased off the remaining vultures and grabbed

some bones, which they hurriedly carried away to munch to destruction in a safer place.

Hyenas are effective scavengers, able to crush the bones that others cannot destroy. Moreover, they are effective hunters. However, their organizational strategy is completely different from that of the vultures. Hyenas have very sophisticated social communities, 'clans' that protect a range. The clan has a strict hierarchy, restricted breeding opportunities, and provides mutual support in defense and hunting.

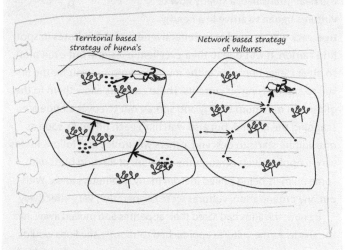

Figure 3.1: Hyena strategy vs vulture strategy in collecting carrion.

Jck and Caroline remained at the kill till the excitement started to recede, and no more animals appeared. The cape buffalo had disappeared; all that was left was a skull, a spine, and a large red spot in the grass.

While driving back, Jack's thoughts had started to wander again, to the previous evening's email about the issues in the innovation department. There appeared to be a link to the difference between vultures and hyenas.

How connecting to a crowd of innovators can balance the predictability of revenue streams and costs

Jack and Caroline only had a small sandwich for late breakfast. The sight of the vultures at the carcass had diminished their appetite. With a cup of tea, they settled at the now familiar spot in front of their tent. After some reminiscing about their holiday experience so far, Jack pulled out his laptop to continue his train of thought from the morning.

Daniel's team had been established to improve output and attract more young and entrepreneurial types, in response to earlier disappointment with the company's ability to create timely innovations that had real impact.

However, the problems around innovation were bigger than the performance of this team. The real worry was that, for three years already, the innovation department had built new funnel models, gates, and innovation processes, but in those same three years all major innovation had originated outside the industry, from young new firms.

How was it possible that his team, staffed by some of the most experienced people in town, was unable to outperform a bunch of campus startups? Even now, despite having copied the startup model, the results were still disappointing.

It was clear to him that the average startup was not necessarily performing better, as he had seen dozens of them come and go. Most of them did not survive. That said, the startup scene as a whole was outperforming his well-organized innovation department, as well as his in-house startup initiative.

So far, they had been able to scramble enough resources and market power to prevent any promising new innovation from building up a position before running out of cash. But surely this was not sustainable. Jack felt vulnerable. Recently, a promising startup, which had developed a surface coating for better cleaning, had been acquired by a metal firm that, even if it was not direct competition, would give the new company access to sufficient funds to achieve a defensible position before the owner ran out of patience, i.e. a great opportunity to scale up.

If only Jack new where to target innovation: Cleaning surfaces? Home automation? Remote monitoring? Energy conservation? Recycled components?

He knew that any of these subjects, as well as many others, could generate huge disruption in their industry. They all needed attention. But how could he address all these issues, let alone innovation in areas that he could not even conceive of today?

Jack and his leadership team had regularly concluded that innovation would enhance M&S's retail position, creating free marketing as well as protecting the firm from external disruption. But how should he reinvigorate his innovation function in the company if he did not even know where the next bonanza would come from?

With a continued sense of unease about this situation, he drifted back to the game drive of that morning, and in particular to the scavengers that had arrived after the lions had eaten their fill. They had strikingly different ways of organizing themselves. Highly socially organized hyenas were akin to his highly organized innovation department, with funnel models and a review committee, versus the anarchic vultures, like the crowd of startups, hovering above his industry, ready to strike whenever a bountiful opportunity arose.

As in the savannah, both organizational models – that of the hyenas and that of the vultures – have their merits in the specific situations that these animals encounter.

Hyenas live within stable ranges, competing with other predators, but especially with other hyena clans. They retain the females born into the clan. By restricting the right to propagate solely to the alfa female, the numbers are managed, and genetic similarity is kept high, which is important for ensuring that all animals are willing to risk life and limb for the whole group. Being in a larger group strengthens the clan's ability to defend the territory against other clans. The bigger the better. As long as there is enough food in an area that can be covered by one group, it makes sense to grow the size of the clan. The group only needs to disperse if food runs out, and then the advantage is lost. If the group becomes too big, individuals might have a better chance of successful propagation by striking out alone.

Hyena structure might be a metaphor for a well-structured firm with a lot of direct competition in an established industry. Size does matter in such industries. These kinds of firms tend to grow until they hit the limits of anti-trust law. All employees in such firms are expected to support each other to operate within a well-defined framework, established by the firm.

Individual vultures float around in areas where the availability of carrion is not very stable. The way herds move through the landscape, the way the predators make kills that leave a carcass, and the way animals die of natural causes, is hard to predict in a single small area. By jointly covering a larger area, vultures benefit from each other's vision to spot opportunities far away.

Even though vultures compete for food at a carcass, the chances of a single individual finding a meal in a day decreases if the number of vultures declines.

Vultures achieve a high level of cooperation without social organization. This cooperation does not require family ties either. They work together as a set of independent players in a network with some engagement rules that drive cooperation.

By working together in this way, vultures cover a vast area and can respond flexibly to an unexpected local abundance of carrion. By gathering in huge numbers shortly after a kill, they can ensure that they claim a substantial part of any major opportunity, regardless of where it appears.

The network of vultures is a good paradigm for the crowd of startups Jack is up against, with a large collection of innovators continuously scanning opportunities. As soon as a new technological breakthrough appears, such as the arrival of a new phone, a new ability to connect devices, new materials, etc., the community generates huge amounts of small, lean startups that can easily outnumber any larger, deep-pocketed R&D department, both in terms of numbers and with respect to agility and low overheads.

Corollary 12: The density and predictability of revenue pools determine the optimal organization pattern in innovation. If predictability is low, large and concentrated players may not be suitably organized to survive.

Jack also recognized a big dilemma for crowd-based entrepreneurs. As soon as a valuable opportunity is found, the environment switches to a much more stable one. If a spot on the savannah started to generate a reliable source of carrion, the vulture model would collapse, as all vultures would be hanging around this place and competition would increase. At this stage, the vultures would benefit from working in larger or organized in groups. If a startup manages to scale up faster than any competitor, they can thrive by switching quickly to a classic incumbent position.

The crowd-based/startup competitive model only works as long as it has not become hugely successful. As soon a big opportunity is found, size matters again. Jack could recall many examples of fights for dominance in new industries.

Ostrich vs secretary bird – Only invest in innovations that have a reasonable likelihood of survival

Jack and Caroline decided on a change of scenery. They spent the afternoon on a shaded veranda on the other side of the camp, shielded from the heat of the day. The veranda offered a great view of the terrain away from the river, grassland with the occasional acacia tree. There was not too much going on, so they chatted away, only occasionally scanning the surroundings. As they poured another cup of tea, they spotted a large male ostrich accompanied by over thirty chicks. It passed a tree in which a secretary bird had built a large nest. Jack pondered the different chick-raising strategies that these birds adopt.

The nesting approach of the secretary bird is quite common among birds. The secretary bird invests in a safe nest at the top of a high, thorny tree. It only produces one or two chicks and invests heavily in these chicks, providing shelter, protection, and a continuous flow of food, largely consisting of snakes or lizards. A single chick has a reasonably high chance of survival, so it is worth the energy invested as there is a high chance of a return on this investment.

As the ostrich cannot fly, a strategy of building a high nest protected from intruders is impossible. The environment in which an ostrich chick grows up is much more uncertain. Investing a lot in a few chicks is a risky strategy that might not pay off. Jack knew that these thirty ostrich chicks are the offspring of many females, clustered together. They are protected, as far as possible, by the father. The ostrich errs toward a low-investment strategy, not feeding the chicks, or keeping them in a

protected area, instead investing its energy in producing more eggs. This ensures that some chicks will survive, even if predation strikes the family many times, as it is likely to. The ostrich strategy is much more suited to the uncertain environment of a ground dweller.

Jack recalled the paper he had read on r/K selection theory. It might be outdated but he found the concept highly attractive. It suggests that, in an uncertain environment, animals will invest in quantity of offspring, rather than quality of care. 'This has a great parallel to innovation in business.' he realized. In a stable business environment, it made sense to place huge bets on product innovation or production capacity. In a more fluid environment, or in the early stages of the innovation funnel, it made more sense to create a large set of small best on potential innovations, and see which innovation succeeds.

How to focus on the right time to switch from a laissez-faire to an intensive care approach for innovation with startups

Jack concluded that there is more to raising good innovative initiatives than organizing a crowd. The company still has to decide what opportunity to invest in.

Just like the organization model, the right level of investment is determined by the chance of a substantial return. The outcome is more unpredictable very early on in the innovation process. The hands off, crowd-based ostrich strategy might be more suitable here.

However, once the innovation has proven itself to have more potential, the chances of success increase. At some stage, it makes sense to start investing more and switching to the secretary bird model.

Jack jumped back to his thinking of that morning, as soon as there is a higher chance of return, it is important for a startup to switch mode to be able to appropriate as much value as possible from the innovation, before others swoop in.

Corollary 13: The success of a startup is not just determined by the high-profile innovation phase, but more so by the ability to grow rapidly and dominate competition in a new niche, at which time an investor or partner can intensify the relationship.

Jack believed that he should focus his attention on this infliction point, or, even better, just before this infliction point. How could he start nurturing potential startups that were on the verge of success? Surely, these startups would become more confident if they saw their chances improving? How should he bring these candidates into the M&S sphere without getting into a bidding war with other interested parties? What would be the most valuable investment in these scaleups to maximize the chance of success?

In the midst of his conundrum, the familiar face of Mike appeared to fetch the Matthews for their evening drive.

Trees and weavers birds – Investment in the crowd makes them want to nest close to you

The couple set out on a drive to the hills in the east, to look for klipspringers. After the excitement of the morning, the evening was an anticlimax. Jack wondered where all the animals had gone. When they saw some impala males having a skirmish they decided to stop and enjoy the sight of the savannah in the setting sun light. They stood next to a tree, which supported a weaver nest. In the southern Africa, Jack had seen single structures with nests the size of a small car. Here, the nests were separate balls, the size of a grapefruit, hanging from the branches by the hundreds.

Jack tried to understand the fate of this tree. Despite having so many of its branches occupied by nests, rather than leaves, it looked quite healthy, certainly healthier than similar trees nearby. Possibly, the continuous presence of birds reduced the number of insects munching away at it leaves. Even more likely, the continuous flow of droppings raining down from the nests was just enough to be beneficial for the tree without killing it. Jack realized that the arrival of the birds might be very favorable for the tree. In other words, the tree that could best attract weaver bird nests greatly enhanced its chances of survival. So, how could a tree ensure that it attracted a flock of weaver birds to its branches? Some factors were not in the tree's control, such as the availability of suitable grass nearby. Other factors, such as the availability of suitable branches at the right height or the thickness of the remaining foliage to protect the nests from the wind, were.

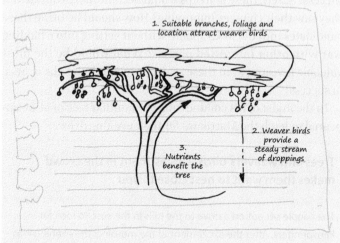

1. Suitable branches, foliage and location attract weaver birds

2. Weaver birds provide a steady stream of droppings

3. Nutrients benefit the tree

Figure 3.2: By giving shelter to weaver bird nests, trees benefit from an increased flow of nutrients.

A tree near suitable grass, with suitable branches, and with the right foliage would stand a much greater chance of successfully attracting a flock.

Jack pulled out his notepad to scribble some notes.

Access to an existing network in an industry is a great base for fostering potential scaleups

If M&S could provide the right environment, foliage, and branches for startups looking to scale up, it could attract flocks of innovation available in the crowd. So, what would these branches and foliage consist of?

Rather than chasing all of the hot developments, Jack would ask the team to develop ways of engaging with and connect to startups with suitable ideas.

By now, the light was fading rapidly so they drove back to the camp.

Jack and Caroline had a quiet evening dinner. Before long, they were sipping tea in front of their tent again, Caroline reading Hemingway's *The Green Hills of Africa*. Jack opened his laptop.

He switched his thoughts back to the issue of his innovation team, which was unable to outpace the industry in terms of speed and functionality. The team was reasonably well funded and placed in a separate environment to avoid too much corporate interference. Despite being the main initiator of this team, he felt slightly apprehensive about the decision to go ahead. To be honest, he had seen smaller, lightly funded startups that he would give a higher chance of coming up with the next big thing.

Even if he was not sure about their performance, what was the alternative? As a leading supplier in the market, he could not abandon innovation altogether.

Buying a startup might be a solution, but which one should he buy? And how could he avoid losing the talent, once they had sold their company and the integration with M&S was in progress. Moreover, this would be a reversion to the 'hyena strategy,' and he had already concluded that, because of the unpredictability of the next big thing, he would be better off with the higher flexibility of the 'vulture strategy' until he had a better idea of the chances of success.

M&S has the highest impact in those innovations that have the best fit with its existing customer base and supplier network. Jack decided to focus on startups with a high level of fit.

He had also concluded that the key phase in the development of a startup would be the stage just before that, when the innovation being pursued starts to attract other parties.

M&S had some valuable resources for scaleups with fit, including its leading position in the industry, its reputation, and its large customer base. M&S could open up these resources to any suitable candidate at little cost.

So, even if M&S could not compete head-to-head with the low-cost frugal organization of the crowd, it can still greatly up the odds of finding a startup at the scaleup stage in its industry.

Because of the low costs involved, M&S could substantially expand the set of candidates without major investment. In this way, it could delay switching from the ostrich strategy to the secretary bird strategy to a later stage in the funnel. At the same time, the startup would already have a much stronger relationship with M&S, increasing the chance of achieving a reasonable agreement for further cooperation.

Corollary 14: A company can effectively attract and select 'best fit' startups by accessing suppliers, partners, and customers. This allows self-selection of multiple candidates, and a delay in the need to direct investment to a lower-risk stage where the relationship is more established.

Jack opened his email and drafted a message for Daniel

Subject: Engaging effectively with the crowd of innovators at the right time

Hi Daniel,

Sorry to hear that our projects are experiencing further delays. I am fully committed to securing M&S's future through innovative new products and solutions, but it seems the current endeavor is not delivering this to the desired level. This is my analysis of the situation:

- We are trying to outrun a large set of small, agile firms that are hugely attractive for entrepreneurial types and risk-seeking investors. Our historic strengths, i.e. reliability, thoroughness, and scale, will prevent us from outperforming this crowd.
- The balance might shift if we focus our effort on the few innovations that make a difference. We could throw our resources behind it. However, we do not yet know which of the many opportunities will be important.
- I have concluded that we are unlikely to change this balance and outcompete the large flock of startups whose owners are working their butts off for free in the hope of becoming billionaires. Most will not survive.
- Instead, let's make sure that those startups that do succeed in creating great products work with us in their go-to-market, and win a great advantage from scaling up.

I want you to take a step back and consider a more open way to innovate, working closely with some of the startups that we have perceived as competitors until now.

- I suggest we go beyond selecting a few ideas or companies, because it will be hard to pick the right ones.
- Also, I do not intend to buy the successful companies, as we would destroy a lot of value when integrating a startup into our more structured organization.
- Instead, I would like M&S to operate as an accelerator that provides an attractive place for startups to execute their go-to-market, and add new features or propositions to our offering. We will let our end customer community select the most attractive ones.
- I think we need to provide some services that make our firm attractive to these startups, to make sure that we attract these firms to our benefit.
- An initial list of services might include:
  - access to our end customer panels to improve their product development
  - connection to our digital functionality
  - visibility of their products in our sales channels
  - a business model that allows both the startup and M&S to benefit
  - access to user data and user satisfaction feedback if possible
  - contact with other teams for cooperation
- We should optimize this cooperation by focusing on attractive growth for those startups that want to scale up, and self-selection rather than early direction. Extra support should only be given further down the chain to those initiatives that prove capable of generating value in our value chain.

Please discuss this new direction with the team and look at how the creative talent can expand this list. I want to make sure that any innovation that is suitable for our industry arrives at our doorstep first!

Let's sit down together next week when I am back, good luck for now,

Regards, Jack

Introduction Chapter 4. Losing cost leadership: The end of the road for efficiency advantages

Jack pushed the send button just as a new email popped up from his CFO, Falik Abgazi.

Hi Jack,

I have picked up from various colleagues that you are having a great time redefining the strategy of our company in the middle of the African bush. As you are on such a creative roll, maybe you can chew over some of the numbers that I have recently been analyzing. We need to get back to basic, and be more careful with these fancy interventions. These new ideas add costs, at a time that our competitiveness is under pressure.

Here are the core numbers I am looking at:

- To maintain a healthy profit level, we need to make 55% gross margin
- We are working with some of the largest producers and lowest prices in the industry. Transparent sustainable sourcing could easily cost us 2.5% margin.
- We are facing tough market conditions, especially in our business with Walmart. Do I need to remind you of their threat to go direct to one of the Chinese suppliers and beat us at our own game?
- The new kid on the block, SunnyFountain, is selling products close to our price point. Without our scale in resourcing, I estimate their margin cannot be more than 45%. This might become a new reality we must get used to, once they increase in size.
- Your latest ideas suggest we start pampering our distributors with investment in 'point of sale' and training, while our competition is going direct at much lower cost. This might add another 2.5% cut in our margin.

In short, our figures don't add up! We could easily face a 10% margin gap. So, before we shoot off in all kinds of new directions, we have to make the numbers work, otherwise we will be forced to abandon these new initiatives halfway, at great cost and risking our reputation for reliable profit generation. Do I need to remind you that, under your uncle, we spent many days shaving costs through tough programs that form the basis of our competitiveness and our past successes? I would hate to see this heritage go up in smoke, chasing new trends that have not proven themselves.

To Jack, this was a familiar tone from Falik. Having already served under Jack's uncle, his predecessor in the family business, he often adopted the role of the protector of the family legacy and Jack always took his counsel very seriously, albeit Falik tended to err on the pessimistic side of things.

He now doubted his own judgment. 'Am I losing sight of reality here in the plains of Africa?' He decided to stop working. Instead, he joined Caroline and a Masai guard for a stroll through the camp, listening to the animals of the night. They finished the day with a smooth whisky back at their tent. As they crawled under the mosquito net, realizing that despite the thoughts of home, they had finally landed in Africa.

4. Supply chain competition: Creating localized, personalized, and relevant value leadership

When Jack woke up, that morning it was still dark, chilly, and quiet in the camp. He looked at his clock, it would be an hour and a half before tea and coffee were served before the morning game drive.

His mind picked up the train of thoughts from the day before, and drifted to the history of M&S that Falik had eluded to in his email.

Jack was now the fourth-generation leader in the family's business, which had been handed down from father to son, until his uncle had found himself without suitable heirs, and asked Jack to lead the company.

Taylor

His great-grandfather had started in the time when Frederick Taylor had just introduced his principles of scientific management. By dividing labor into small steps, productivity can be maximized. He had focused on standardization to increase scale, de-skilling the steps of the production process, enabling the employment of low-wage immigrants.

This was at the time when Ford had built his first production chains, producing 'any color so long as it is black.' In those days, M&S had become a medium-size, fully integrated company, buying raw materials in bulk, and executing all aspects of production in-house.

By adopting these 'modern' management practices, the firm had set a precedent in its history, always trying out new management practices and incorporating what works.

Even during the life of his great-grandfather, however, cracks appeared in the scientific model, the competitiveness of highly deskilled, standardized production methodologies. As wealth increased, so did the demand for greater product variation, and not just with respect to function, but also design. It became increasingly attractive for firms to make smaller batches with different designs or specifications, compensating for the loss in efficiency with a much higher sales price. Large, multi-step, Taylor-inspired production processes have the tendency to create some waste between each step and are not very flexible. When his grandfather took on the leadership role, M&S was losing business.

Sociotechnology

Jack's grandfather had been a keen follower of sociotechnology, to optimize the production of smaller, more diversified batches of products. As Jack grew up, his grandfather had shared stories on the subject, such as the Tavistock experiment in the Durham mines in the UK.

Historically, in a coal mine, planning and control was executed above ground, at the start of each shift. This is far away from the working environment, a few hundred meters underground, a working environment that might generate new circumstances every hour.

In the mid-twentieth century, the Tavistock Institute of Human Relations evaluated an alternative approach. In that famous case, the organization of the mine shifted from a classic Taylorian approach, with three specialized shifts, toward self-governing shifts that could react flexibly to changing circumstances underground. Key to the success is the creation of multi-skilled shifts (teams). The planning, control, and incentives are shifted to the coalface, the place where decision-making is most informed, responses can be managed most effectively, and response times are lowest.

His grandfather had invested in training staff. He had set up self-governing teams, making the production better able to cope with the more frivolous demands of the 1950s and 60s

Lean manufacturing & globalization

At the time that Jack's uncle had taken the helm at M&S, the Japanese were conquering the world with manufactured products, in particular electronics and cars. His uncle had travelled to Japan to find out for himself what was happening. In line with the company's heritage, he fully embraced the lean methods of the Japanese manufacturing industry. However, the increasing efficiency of production could not prevent the need to outsource some production of components to low-labor-cost countries, such as Mexico and, later, China. Components were increasingly produced by specialized firms with huge efficiencies of scale, closely linked via supply chain networks, producing on demand, just in time.

The combination of increased specialization and scale had caused a continuous drop in the costs of manufacturing a product. Much of this saving had gone to end customers, but a substantial part had been invested in branding and marketing.

By the time Jack had taken over from his uncle, the firm was a market leader as a result of its scale in production, distribution, and mass marketing. It was able to remain cost leader in its market, and its branded products sold at a decent premium. At the time, it seemed that Jack was going to have an easy ride till the next handover, but as Falik's email showed, the once unassailable bastion was coming under siege.

Loss of scale advantage

Jack tried to sort the developments to see how he could explain the loss of competitive advantage that was occurring despite their market position. It was clear that M&S is not in a position to claim the kind of scale advantages that some large tech companies have, advantages that often border on the edge of monopolies. Instead, Jack focused on the operating environment for any normal-sized company in direct competition:

- The function of the article is a small and decreasing part of its value. As customers are increasingly affluent, they value exclusivity, a story, personalization and/or local content. The production costs of standard components become a smaller part of the customer selling price, the remainder being increasingly filled with other value for the customer, such as brand, personalization, installation, personal service, and experience. These are often local and are not subject to the same scale advantages.
- As supply chains become sets of highly efficient specialists, any firm with some volume can competitively source the same quality products. Much of M&S's scale advantage in the production of items now rests in its supply chain. This has created a dynamic, competitive supplier market for parts and subassemblies, available for every step of the supply chain in many industries. A firm that wanting to start a new product line can easily tap into this supplier ecosystem. It faces much lower initial investment or hurdles to building capacity. These items, produced at large scale, are available to every firm at only slightly higher costs, often via international trade shows, AliExpress, and other online players.
- With the arrival of Amazon and marketplaces, any firm has direct access to the whole market at roughly comparable costs. Distribution to customers was opening via the likes of Amazon, allowing smaller firms to get instant national distribution at very competitive cost levels.

Jack was glad that he was not in an industry that was subject to an even more drastic shift in cost structure, in the form of crowd sourcing, such as hotels or taxis, where the assets are spare capacity provided by consumers or small entrepreneurs.

By now, Caroline was starting to stir. He finished his notes, closed his laptop, and looked at his wife, gently waking up, and handed her a cup of tea.

Alliance of wildebeest and grass – Competition is more effective at ecosystem level

That morning, they decided to take another trip to the Mara River crossing. As they approached the river, they found some smaller herds of wildebeest, which did not stop to forage but were tracking in long lines to the Mara plains. The herds that had previously passed by had obviously affected the landscape. As Jack scanned the plain from the car, he observed the difference from the area close to the camp. Here, the large herds had passed in such great numbers that they had eaten every juicy leaf of grass available before moving on to new pastures. With the grass largely gone, there was little left for the remaining sedentary antelope to do but to strip down the remaining bushes till the last leaf. This scarcity of food would exert a tremendous downward pressure on the numbers of sedentary antelopes that compete with wildebeest for browsing. It would also prevent any shrub from growing taller and becoming out of reach for most browsers, as it would already have been completely stripped. By the time the rain comes, there will be nothing left, as most bushes will have been decimated by the sedentary browsers. At that stage, the grass will have the benefit of being able to grow rapidly from the root systems that remain intact, with very little competing leaves blocking the sunlight.

It was clear how the grass benefitted the moving herds, allowing for a concentrated intake of fodder, supporting the requirements of the herd. These herds, in turn, are eating grasses, but are even worse for bushes. In the competition of grass vs bush, these herds benefitted the position of grasses. By forcing the browsing of shrubs, the area remains open, which means grass can appropriate most of the sunlight when the rains return.

'This was not matter of wildebeest competing with impala, or grass competing with bushes,' Jack realized, 'it was a matter of the wildebeest-grass system competing with the impala-bush system.' What Jack observed around him was competition between ecosystems for a limited supply of space, sun energy, and nutrients. That is how wildebeest and grass work together to jointly push out the impala and the shrubs. At the same time, they are creating an ecosystem that has the highest animal biomass per square km in the world.

Corollary 15: Competition can be avoided by promoting an ecosystem that is unsuitable for the competitors.

Within the ecosystem, the wildebeest can appropriate much of the resources. As ruminants, they are more efficient digesters of fodder than zebra. Compared to the Thomson gazelle, they are larger, tracking earlier, forcing the Thomson gazelle toward lower, leftover leaves. This is the ecological equivalent of a production supply chain system, with the savannah as a high efficiency animal biomass generator, where the wildebeest take the lion's share.

This system has some prerequisites, including a periodic drought. In climates that provide a more constant supply of water, growth continues throughout the year. The sedentary population is not forced to strip down the bushes, leading to the survival of trees and, in the long term, the transition to forests.

Jack made a sketch of these ideas.

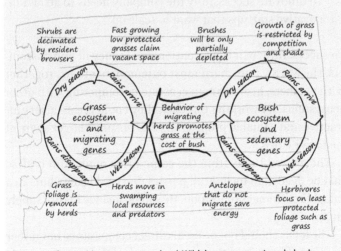

Figure 4.1: Competition at ecosystem level: Wildebeest-grass vs impala-bush

During the drive back to the camp, Jack applied the idea of competing ecosystems to his business environment.

He began to consider shifting his focus: From focus on production costs to a focus on competitiveness in the value chain. He replaced the limited availability of space, sun, and nutrients, with the limited availability of customer money to spend. He evaluated how M&S, together with other parties in the value chain, such as suppliers and resellers, could best compete for customers' money.

How cooperation within an ecosystem opens up opportunities for more effective competition.

Jack's conclusion from the previous days started to converge toward a common theme of smart cooperation with others:

- For successful marketing, M&S needed the cooperation of its direct and end customers.
- To avoid a price spiral, the firm must work together with its distributors to provide a rich proposition
- To innovate successfully the company needs to attract innovative startups that want to scale up

To successfully win the attention and money of end customers, the M&S value chain must outcompete others, together with partners, in a common ecosystem, competing with other ecosystems. By working together, they could create a very attractive and valuable proposition, and ensure a larger share of customer euros.

The grazed fields from the game drive made him realize that he needed to include all parties that could contribute to a valuable customer proposition. He should include his full supply chain.

The focus should not be on his direct competitors, but rather on other offers where customers can spend their euros.

Lunch with the Agnelli's: Enabling your partners to contribute helps tackle cost issues

As Jack and Caroline had made a long drive that morning, they found the breakfast area almost empty when they returned. They decided to join the only remaining couple. It took little time to establish that he was a physician, she led Coronara, a firm that makes heart monitors. Jack relished the opportunity to explore this unfamiliar business.

The market for heart monitoring used to be split between hospital-based analysis, often quite extensive, and more simple home monitoring devices. Coronara focused on the latter. Unsurprisingly, the heart monitoring business was a growing but very competitive market, with a wide array of suppliers, large branded electronic firms, small niche health firms, and many decent quality low-cost suppliers from China.

As he explored Coronara's situation a bit further, however, it turned out that their biggest headache was not these low-cost producers. Coronara's strength in home monitoring, based on a patented sensor technology, had enabled it to protect its market share against low-end suppliers. The real disruption came from the merging of professional and home services.

The market for heart monitors is just a small part of the market for heart monitoring and related health advice. Fitness clubs have started to provide heart monitoring with training advice. Pharmacies have started to provide blood pressure and heart monitoring with advice on nutritional supplements. The heart monitor cost is such a small part of the total consumer spend in such places that, often, the analysis is given away for free to create traffic. It is hard to compete with a free alternative offer.

Coronara had responded by teaming up with family doctors. This was not an obvious move as family doctors perceived Coronara encouraging consumers to check themselves at home as a big threat to their business. Coronara provided a new proposition, a monitor that a consumer connects to their PC or mobile to upload data to a personal vault, managed by Coronara. A consumer can grant access

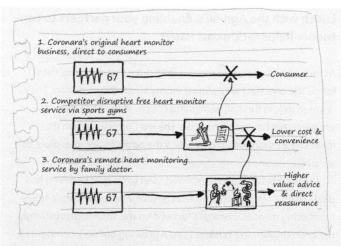

1. Coronara's original heart monitor business, direct to consumers

⎍⋀⋀⋀ 67 ──────────── ✕ ➤ Consumer

2. Competitor disruptive free heart monitor service via sports gyms

⎍⋀⋀⋀ 67 ──────────── ➤ [gym/checklist] ⧓ ✕ ➤ Lower cost & convenience

3. Coronara's remote heart monitoring service by family doctor.

⎍⋀⋀⋀ 67 ──────────── ➤ [doctor] ➤ Higher value: advice & direct reassurance

Figure 4.2: Doctor ecosystem vs sports gym ecosystem: How Coronara disrupts the disrupter.

to a family doctor, allowing them to evaluate the home measurements during a consultation. The vaults had created a small extra revenue stream for Coronara but, more importantly, they had reasserted the home as the place to do regular monitoring. Even more profound was the effect on family doctors, who saw the solution as a way to reclaim some of their business from pharmacy chains.

Additionally, Coronara had acquired a service firm to maintain and approve the monitors, creating another revenue stream. Coronara was doing very well now. As the cost of the monitor was a small part of the total revenue stream, it could aggressively fight back any low-cost price competitors with budget models.

As breakfast spilled over into lunch and on to tea, the Matthews found the Agnellis to be very pleasant company. They were sorry to hear that the Agnellis were leaving for Amboseli the next morning.

How Coronara, as the ecosystem enabler, is winning the battle for creating value for the end customer

Jack returned to their tent energized. He decided to spend some time in the front compartment organizing his thoughts on the day's events.

He reflected on the similarities between the wildebeest promoting grass and Coronara promoting family doctors, both interacting in a way that meant the combination would prevail.

All herbivores are in a constant struggle to outcompete others for acquisition of essential nutritional building blocks, such as proteins and energy. The success of the wildebeest is determined by the resources that can be claimed for their bodies and indirectly by the propagation of those plants that are most suitable for their constitution. Wildebeest do not just compete head on with other herbivores by trying to be smarter, faster, or better digesters, they also appropriate the largest share of available nutrition by promoting an ecosystem and dependencies that favor it in competition with other herbivores. They regularly overgraze an area, to the extent that those plants that can best cope with being trimmed down regularly are promoted, at the cost of plants/trees that are less resistant. Wildebeest provide an essential service to these plants, at hardly any cost to themselves.

For Coronara, the ecosystem consisted of the company supply chain as well as the sales and service channels to consumers. Other ecosystems, such as health clubs and pharmacies, were seeking to appropriate the same consumer euros. By giving family doctors access to the measurements online, Coronora was promoting a beneficial ecosystem for itself, at hardly any cost. At the same time, it avoids the consumer spend flowing to alternative ways of monitoring health, where Coronara is less well positioned.

Another remark by the Agnellis had stuck in the back of Jack's head. 'The low-cost Chinese imports were not an issue'. He could now see that the value that Corona is creating consisted of very effective complete health monitoring and improving the ability of doctors to provide the right treatment. The cost of a heart monitor is only a very small part of this 'rich' proposition. Reducing the costs of the monitor is negligible in the full costs of the service for the end consumer.

Corollary 16: Focus should not be on how to build a supply chain most cost effectively. Instead, attention should focus on the value chain, creating superior value by enlisting networks of local resources to add to the experience, the personalization, and the completeness of the product and service.

By enlisting the help of a network or a crowd of doctors, Coronara is creating a level of local relevance and personalization that is exactly the kind of brand value he was looking for on day one.

'How could this be applied to M&S? What would a very rich value chain for end customers look like?,' he wondered. M&S was not in the medical business; still, its products were more than just pieces of metal or plastic. The most attractive value chain is the one that produces 'rich' value in the most effective way. As 'rich' value is personalized and experience-focused, it often requires the responsive contribution of people and local situational connection. By sourcing this service through networks of related professionals, partners, or end customers, this personalized service can be delivered in a very responsive and competitive way.

Jack thought of some subjects that would influence customer satisfaction, besides the product itself:

- Instructions and use: Anything that facilitated the setup, installation, or use of their product would greatly enhance the value that an end customer would get out of it. Maybe there are parties that have great digital tools to improve these. Or a network of handymen or professional customers that can support installation and first use.
- Experience: People are keen to get new ideas about using the product. Or to share their experiences or tricks of their trade. Or to find info on experienced professionals using their products. Or even sharing their use with others in their neighborhood.

- Efficient acquisition. Anything that reduces the effort required for a customer to acquire the product is valuable, including physical access or delivery, but also making it easy to select the right product or the right version.
- Personalized products: Customers would love to have their own, personally designed product. Or a product customized for their own situation. Perhaps local shops or craftsman could take the basic M&S product and augment it with a personal touch.

Jack realized that there was a wealth of value to be delivered around the product that could potentially be sourced via a network of local actors. However, the reverse is also true. If others claim a strong position in terms of delivering this value, the role of M&S could soon be that of a commodity supplier to such a network. Even if M&S invests in developing such a network, how could it ensure it would not lose it to a low-cost Chinese rival once it was established? He saw no opportunity for a cloud solution like Coronara.

As Jack was processing his thoughts, it started to dawn on him how profound the change to the value network was.

As customers increasingly spent their euros on products that are exclusive, are customized, are personalized, and with a personal story, a lower share of the spend goes to the core product. Even if there is an opportunity for highly cost effective sourcing, this does not drive the competitiveness of the complete value network. Service has become an increasingly large part of the cost price and the value.

As the core product share decreases, production cost advantages become less critical of overall competitiveness. Rather, the ability to add value through personalized specification, a touch of hand crafting, local presence, and/or sustainability are crucial to being competitive. In all these fields, small-scale producers have a strong advantage. The ability to defend an industry based on scale is disappearing.

If M&S wants to run the 'rich' value stream, it needs to compete with a highly complex value network. Falik was right to identify that this could not be competitively done with the current way that M&S is operating. It would not stand a chance against competing networks that utilize modern, competitive ways of organizing value creation.

Just as this worrying thought crossed his mind, Caroline poked him in his side, smiling: 'You look like you have seen a ghost. It's time to hit the dirt road again, and come back to earth'.

Ant soldiers on acacia trees: To make partners work for you, you must provide them with a benefit

That evening, Jack and Caroline decided to drive a short distance east, toward the slopes that form the eastern edge of the Masai Mara game reserve.

As they drove, the landscape changed from open grass plains to more bush and wood-like growth of small trees. The landscape became increasingly rugged as they climbed, enjoying beautiful views over the plains. After an hour's drive, they stopped near a ridge to have a snack.

They were alone, in the quiet bush. No bleating of herds to be heard. Only the occasional noise from a flock of guinea fowl disturbing the total peace. Caroline decided to take a small stroll through the trees, but Mike jumped up and cautioned her. He pointed at the bulb-like growth at the root of the thorns in the small whistling thorn trees that surrounded them. 'These bulbs are hollow and house aggressive ants. Their bites hurt quite badly'.

The bulbs had developed as a defense
in the battle between trees and herbivores. The acacias have not invested their energy in making more or longer thorns, or in higher trunks, but instead in shelter for ants, as a very effective defense against unwanted guests. They attack insects that eat the leaves, they attack larger herbivores, and they even destroy siblings of new trees that might compete with their 'home' tree.

This protection does not come for free. Besides the costs in energy to create the bulbs, the ants do protect some unwanted guests like aphids that suck fluids from the leaves and spread diseases to the trees. The acacias constantly moderate the balance between the cost of the ants and the risk from browsing. As the number of browsers increases, these trees make more bulbs. If the amount reduces, they reduce the number of bulbs.

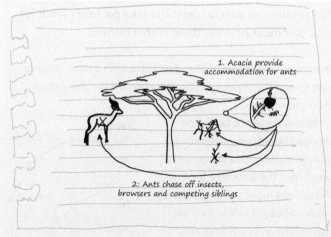

Figure 4.3: Acacia provides lodging and food for its ant protectors and gets protection in return.

Caroline was careful to steer clear of the branches as she walked to the edge. She spent some time taking photographs of the view. They enjoyed the peaceful atmosphere of the lunch spot, until they decided to drive back. On the way back, they were lucky enough to come across a honey badger, a sturdy abnormality in the savannah.

How customers can be a low-cost source of value creation for the value chain

By the time they arrived at the camp, the sun was setting. After dinner, Jack looked at his earlier three emails on branding, distribution, and innovation. Now, these had been added to by the fourth issue of the competitive value chains. Reflecting on the whistling thorn, Jack realized a common theme was developing. In each of the aspects he found the need to better support parties in the network or even end customers, to leverage their contribution to the total value created by the firm.

- Brands

Brands increasingly create value between customers, rather than value between company and customer. They support peer-to-peer communication that reinforces social belonging. The role of communication from company to client diminishes as companies become more transparent. Its brand-specific content is replaced by the content on the firm or product itself.

M&S needs to reduce direct media investment. Instead, it should invest in content and connection that allows for a self-reinforcing message about their company, their brand, their products, and their solutions in general.

- Distribution

Customers have growing choice and control over where to get information, and how to select and acquire goods or services. They will only select a sales channel if it provides superior value through efficiency, effectiveness, reduced risk, and engagement.

M&S needs to work closer with retailers to build in-store experiences that fit flawlessly into the total journey that an end customer makes toward acquiring an M&S product.

- Innovation

Innovation moves toward the crowd as the barriers to innovating are reduced through the availability of shared services. The remuneration structure of the crowd is more suitable for the highly talented entrepreneurial, free-thinking people that typically drive innovation.

M&S needs to focus its R&D on the core functionality of the product. Functionality around the product, such as connectivity, new services, new payment options, mobile-assisted installation, use, or maintenance can be left to a much larger crowd of startups, that develop such ideas in a community.

- Supply chain

Product value is increasingly created in the last mile, e.g. the personalization, installation, service, localization, and augmentation around the product for the specific needs of the customer.

M&S needs to leverage its size over the different personalization agents, by making its products suitable for such localization as well as sharing knowledge and leads, supporting 'localizers'' performance.

Jack decided that M&S needed to become more like the whistling thorns, providing a platform, enabling end customers and maybe other partners to create value, rather than building an ever-expanding integrated company.

> *Corollary 17: Customers are an important and growing part of the value chain, as they create brand value, match products to requirements, localize and customize, and jointly decide on what they think is or is not valuable.*

Subject: Switching attention to value to solve cost issues in the supply chain

Hi Falik,

Thank you for your honest and direct email regarding the decline in our margin structure. I understand that my recent proposals for investing in retail partners, improving sustainability, and increasing online presence may appear to exacerbate the decline in competitiveness, however, I assure you, that this is not the case.

As you know, I am proud of the way we are managing our business based on a limited set of KPIs related to topline, costs, and margin. However, it seems that while we're constantly fighting to remain at the forefront of the benchmarks, we are less successful in defending our profitability.

- Products become ubiquitous, pressure from large retailers and e-tailers create downward pressure on prices.
- Costs that are associated with maintaining our position are increasing. Some costs seem to become hygiene factors, rather than growth drivers, such as advertising, sustainable sourcing, and the faster update of our products.
- We also seem to be outflanked by new players that do not focus on these cost- and margin-related KPIs at all.

It is because of these concerns in particular that I am entertaining the new thoughts you have picked up on. To remain profitable, we must change focus. We need to develop strategies based on these insights:

- *Our biggest threat comes from outside our ecosystem, e.g. other ways for end customers to spend money. Unless we find ways to keep our industry attractive, we are bound to become a commodity player, a role that we will not succeed in without sacrificing much of what our company stands for.*
- *This means that to stay successful we must defend the attractiveness of the proposition of our whole industry, not just our position in the industry.*
- *An attractive industry does not compete on costs, but rather on value.*
- *If we provide the full package, end customers are willing to spend their euros with us. The package must include the experience at the time of acquiring our product, the use of it, and sharing the pleasure of using it.*
- *Personalization of the product and personal service greatly enhance the value of our proposition. This means that end customers will not get better value for money by us shaving a few percentage points of the cost price.*
- *We need to ensure that we link seamlessly to a network of local service providers who efficiently augment the product, the service, and the total experience.*
- *We can thrive in such a network if we make it more efficient, more effective, and if we create a strong hold on its members.*
- *As the leading company in our industry, we can take advantage of our size and scale to create a more attractive and profitable network for partners. By expanding our network and diversifying our offerings to be more localized, we can attract more partners and invest in the network more efficiently.*

In sum, to stay profitable, we must switch our focus from creating the most cost-effective supply chain to creating the most attractive value creation network for end customers, partners, and resellers.

As you have correctly gasped, this requires new initiatives that cost money.

- *For example, to attract valuable partners to our network we have to offer them a benefit, 'a share of the pie,' which cannot always be offset by higher prices.*
- *Moreover, if we use a digital network to build these relations, we must invest in such a system, and the acquisition of partners.*

There are also savings to be made, as we do not have to do all aspects of the value creation ourselves. We can abort the flagship stores, cancel the high-cost mass media investment, and halt some of our own innovation projects.

Overall, we can be more effective if we optimize our value network to create value more efficiently, simultaneously not trying to do everything ourselves, creating room for profitability on those contributions to the network that we continue to make.

What I would like you to do is to put some meat on these bones:

- *First, expand our current supply chain analysis to include all monetary and non-monetary ways that value is created for end customers of our products.*
- *Based on this analysis, we should create a benchmark that includes our end customers, our retail partners, and our professional customers as alternative ways to produce the value.*
- *We can then compare their performance with the value network of our competition. Our KPIs should focus on continuously driving the efficiency and effectiveness of our value network.*

Here are some initial ideas on the components of this network. I shared the first three ideas earlier during this trip:

- *Engaging end customers to create peer-to-peer brand value*
- *Enlisting selected dealers to create a superior acquisition experience*
- *Attracting small innovative startups to provide innovation in our proposition*

In addition, the service delivery and experience around the product can be delivered through such a network, avoiding costs that would normally land in the supply chain.

By designing and producing our products as a flexible foundation that can be augmented by our value network, we can involve smaller contributors to augment this base and offer greater value to our end customers. This approach allows for a more diverse range of offerings and increased customization for our end customers, without the associated costs, i.e.:

- End customers can make themselves available to answer questions and give service in return for benefits we provide, such as accreditation or discounts on reusable products.
- Professional customers can give courses or organize events to create extra revenue or add to their local end-customer base.
- Local producers or garage-based 'makers' can create personalized versions of our products, with different designs or that are suitable for specific applications.

Let's jointly explore if the sums add up. If they do, then the transformation of our supply chain is even more urgent and profound.

To start the exercise, could you follow the above-mentioned steps:

1. Focus on all sources of value associated with the product.
2. Expand to include all possible contributors to this value.
3. Choose most competitive mode of creating the value.

To conclude, it is not that I have lost my appetite for cost effectiveness, it is just that the rules of the game have changed, which forces me explore these new ways of doing business.

Regards,

Jack

Introduction Chapter 5: How to tie all the ideas together?

Jack heard the familiar ping as he pressed the send button. He noticed that there were no new pressing emails in his mailbox, giving him an opportunity to contemplate how to execute the ideas of the last four days in a more cohesive manner. Perhaps he could ask Carla from the strategy department to give Falik a hand, but he decided that, first, he should structure his thoughts further. With this plan in mind, he closed his laptop and enjoyed the rest of the evening chatting with Caroline and re-reading a book he had devoured in his younger years: *The Selfish Gene* by Richard Dawkins.

5. Platform company: Designing a platform to achieve a sustainable competitive position

Distant view at the Ngoro-Ngoro – Each step of the value chain should adapt to the dynamism of the environment

The next morning, Jack and Caroline set out early for a hot air balloon safari. Jack was not very keen on these safaris as he preferred the intimate contact with nature of the trips by jeep, but the promise of a stunning view of the migrating herds had changed his mind and they settled on a no-frills trip (unlike the popular trips with champagne breakfast) to the south of the game reserve, close to the border with Tanzania.

Once in the air, the view was truly breathtaking. Huge herds of wildebeests snaked through the landscape. They also got a beautiful overview of the landscape, both the Masai Mara and the Serengeti.

Jack and Caroline discussed the many features that they could distinguish with the guide. He named the different rivers crossing the plains. He showed them the mountains to the east of the Serengeti, where many of the vultures of the plains would have their nests. In the distance, they could just distinguish the edge of the Ngoro-Ngoro crater. The guide pointed to the plains next to this old volcano. That is where the wildebeest have their calves. The old volcanic deposits provide a nutrient-rich soil for grass, in turn providing nutrient-rich food for wildebeest at the time they need it the most, when suckling their newborn calves.

In the current season, though, the area is desolate. Only the area inside the crater still has significant numbers of wildebeest present.

On previous trips, Jack and Caroline had visited the crater itself. It is a small paradise, closed off from the rest of the plains by a steep ridge, with only a small opening to the southwest. A micro ecosystem with abundant wildlife all year round. The Ngoro-Ngoro also contains small herds of wildebeest; however, most of these do not migrate.

As they floated further over the landscape and enjoyed the spectacle, Jack's thoughts lingered on this fact. The same species of wildebeest would migrate in one place and be sedentary in another. Jack had always thought that the behavior of animals was somehow genetically determined, with differences between species but shared behavior within species. Yet, this was clearly not the case in wildebeest migration. Some other mechanisms must be at work.

'Why do the Ngoro-Ngoro herds not migrate?', Jack asked the guide. He responded that 'the Wildebeest react to the environment they live in. The herds on the plains benefit from differences in availability of food during the season in different parts of the plains. By moving around, they can always claim the best patches of food in the whole area. The flat plain makes it relatively easy to migrate, and they have the additional benefits of leaving the main predators behind, as they cannot travel when they have young.'

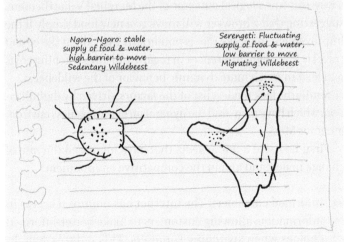

Ngoro-Ngoro: stable supply of food & water, high barrier to move Sedentary Wildebeest

Serengeti: Fluctuating supply of food & water, low barrier to move Migrating Wildebeest

Figure 5.1: Migration of wildebeest in Serengeti vs Ngoro-Ngoro differ as they adapt to different levels of dynamism of their environment.

'The crater environment is much less dynamic. The crater herds have a relatively steady food supply all year around, and migration would involve crossing the narrow crater entrance. The extract they would gain from migration would not outweigh the costs involved'.

Jack explored the line of thought further with the guide, until the guide switched his focus to the landing.

How to match the organizational model of a platform with the dynamism of the environment it addresses

They arrived at the camp just after lunch and decided to only take a short afternoon trip as that evening the head of national parks would visit and give a lecture on his organization. This left Jack with some time to further process his thoughts.

Seeing the wildebeest adjust their way of living and organization to the level of dynamism in their food supply made him wonder about dynamism in the business environment for M&S and how they should respond.

Herd behavior was determined both by stability in the available food supply and the costs of moving around between supplies. In a way, this was a logical outcome of the Marginal Value theorem, suggesting that a browser will move to a new food supply if the improvement in intake rate is potentially high and if the cost of travel is low. High differences in regard and low switching costs will lead to much more dynamic behavior of the wildebeest.

Similarly, Jack made a list of the factors, driven by digitalization, which have increased the dynamism of the business environment for M&S.

First, he listed a few aspects that have increased the rate of change in demand and in the competitive environment:

– Informed customers: The internet has improved access to information, allowing customers to make better-informed choices when switching suppliers. This reduces switching costs for customers and makes company revenue less predictable.

- Peer-to-peer branding: Social interaction online has greatly enhanced the ability of customers to build their own brand value, becoming less dependent on large media campaigns. This means that the potential to forecast or influence future hits has diminished, making the business less predictable.
- Availability of spare assets, such as empty bedrooms or parked cars, and the ability to access these spare assets via internet services, has created new, potentially very cost-effective business models. These can be seen as unpredictable competition, which can have a sudden and huge impact on available business.
- Global supply chain of high-volume, low-cost producers that can be accessed by any buyer effectively make producers less dependent on production base. This is further facilitated by platforms such as AliExpress.
- Business services that facilitate the setup of a new business, such as in marketing (freeware Content management, social marketing), sales (freeware eCommerce, Amazon), distribution (UPS, FedEx), production (3D printing, makers movement), and knowledge (sharing sites for IT problems, legal questions, etc.).

As Jack looked at the list, the message was clear. Digitalization leads to a much more dynamic environment. He now wanted to check whether the suspicion that he had had since he looked at SunnyFountain, a small effective competitor, was right. Is it true that small firms benefit more from this dynamism than large firms? He listed some ways that smaller companies adapt to this dynamic environment:

- Close direct contact with customers allows small companies to predict and manage their demand much better, as opposed to larger companies that must work with intermediate stock and capacity planning.
- As material wealth of customers grows, their desire for personalization and content-heavy products allows small

firms to sell at higher prices points. This allows them to leverage their ability to create smaller, more bespoke and local products.

- Another effect of growing wealth is that workers are increasingly motivated by non-monetary rewards. Many spend their evenings giving free advice, just for the status they receive on a forum. People will happily contribute to local growers and pay a premium to enjoy it.

- Finally, these fragmented industries are much more attractive to talent and capital. A key attraction for both is the chance to hit the jackpot. But the reduced effort required to have a modestly comfortable life and feed the family, as well as the importance of having more control over the choices you make in life, make these firms highly attractive to the most talented employees in the market.

How could M&S systematically respond to this development? Should M&S behave more like the herd on the Serengeti than like the one in the Ngoro-Ngoro crater to remain competitive? Is the role of M&S that of the herd, or is it that of the grass plains?

M&S should not try to switch to dynamism itself. It should enable its suppliers, partners, and end customers to operate more effectively, thus ensuring that a larger part of the end consumer euros would go to their joint ecosystem.

At the same time, M&S should keep leveraging its size and scale.

It was not clear to Jack yet where exactly to focus on more rigid, efficient scale and where the focus should be on small, flexible value creation. It was also not clear which parts of the value chain M&S should take ownership of and which parts should be driven by its partners. That said, the balloon safari had made one design rule clear to him:

Corollary 18: In the more dynamic aspects of the value chain, it makes sense to delegate value creation to partners who can adapt and respond based on their own merits.

Dominant networks – The benefits to candidate participants drive network growth

That afternoon, they drove to a small hill nearby, overlooking the plains, to enjoy the sunset. Herds of zebra were slowly moving through the landscape whilst grazing, only occasionally disturbed by a short outburst of aggression between competing stallions.

It is funny how there is so much grass and space, yet still theses zebras flock together in a small area, competing with other herd members over a small patch. In the zebras case, this behavior was generally thought to protect against predators, but, then again, there are many antelopes that do not live in herds.

One step up the ladder of abstraction, why do many animals flock together? Why do they all choose the same spot?

Jack thought of a few examples that he had seen earlier that week.

If you see a tree full of weaver birds, you can be pretty sure that the trees around it will not attract any. Why would any newly arrived male join the fray and opt for the remaining mediocre branches in an already crowded tree rather than select a nice branch in an empty adjacent tree? Probably because the chance of raising chicks without losing them to predation is higher in an already crowded tree. A nest alone in a tree sticks out as an obvious target. Building a nest and laying eggs takes considerable energy, it is not very efficient to waste this on a spot that is unlikely to get results.

The next example that sprang to mind was the network of vultures. Jack imagined how all vultures would glide around together in a network, all maintaining a similar height. If one vulture flew lower than the others, it might find carrion faster and go undetected when landing. However, this reduced competition would probably not compensate for the loss of carrion detected by others in the same network. So, vultures are obliged to lock on to a network operating at a similar height and with mutual visibility in order to effectively pinpoint carrion.

Another flocking phenomenon that had always puzzled Jack was the way wildebeest cross rivers. Every year, they find a different spot that all of them use. The spot might not be the best place to cross, and often it is not the best location for exiting the water. If the herd moved just a few hundred meters further upstream, they would have a much lower chance of breaking a leg, climbing in or out. However, once the first animals have committed to crossing all others follow suit.

Jack envisaged how any subsequent animal could choose the crossing point. By being adventurous and trying another location, it might find a spot that is much more favorable to crossing, reducing the percentage of animals that drown or that cannot get out on the opposite bank.

These benefits accrue mostly to the animals that follow the adventurous one, whilst the adventurous animal itself runs a much greater risk of dying. By following the herd, an animal knows that the crossing is possible, and that predators may already have fed on the forerunners. Once a crossing is used, it creates a strong lock-in for the whole herd, as the switching costs are much higher than the potential benefit for the switcher.

Jack sketched away in his notebook while enjoying the view and his thoughts in the comfort of the jeep.

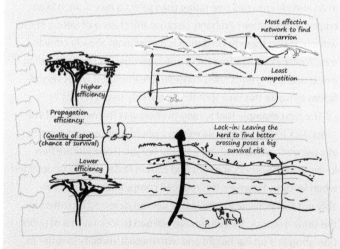

Figure 5.2 Natural examples of winning crowds or networks.

Soon after they arrived back in camp, Jack found himself in his familiar spot in front of his tent with his laptop and a glass of whisky. As he reflected, his thoughts drifted back to the African savannah, the camp, and the more practical challenges of deciding where to go that night. After an early dinner, he and Caroline attended a lecture on national park management by Chief Leopold Mkabe

Corollary 19: A network competes with other networks to attract more participants. Networks must strategize to become preferred, by providing efficiency, effectiveness, or a lock-in for potential participants.

National parks management – A platform company that creates growth of nature, economy, and society

They had encountered Chief Leopold Mkabe previously in the camp and found him to be both visionary and engaging. They were fortunate to have the opportunity to attend his presentation that night. Since Leopold had taken over as the head of the national parks organization, the game reserves had gone experienced a resurgence, with visitor numbers increasing and a halt in the decline of some key species, such as elephant and rhino.

Leopold showed a presentation on the overall situation in the park, focusing in particular on game, visitors, personnel, and neighbors.

Leopold began by highlighting some cases he had been involved in during his tenure at various national parks organizations. He introduced the cases as examples of counterintuitive management decisions, i.e. taking decisions that initially seemed to harm the park's position but which ultimately led to unexpected long-term benefits:

- To improve wildlife survival at times of drought, the park created several drinking pans, with water pumped up from aquifers. However, these pans attracted local herders from outside the park as much as wildlife. This led to more competition for vegetation and the killing of large predators. The park determined that the best way to improve the survival rate of wildlife during droughts was to create additional wells outside the park, close to the dwellings of the herdsmen.

- Some parks were started by bringing in experienced teams from abroad. Even if the core organization benefitted from the experience, the local situation often deteriorated as local villagers only saw an opportunity for additional income through poaching. Some parks actively switched back to hiring more people from the local community, thus creating incentive and leverage to reduce poaching, even if the organization suffered.

- In addition to park fees, revenue from lodges are a main source of income for parks. Some parks manage their own facilities to maximize control and appropriate this revenue. Leopold brought in external entrepreneurs, who had experience within the hotel business. This expertise created a much more interesting and diversified offer. So, even if own lodge income shrunk, overall income from fees went up, as traffic increased substantially. Moreover, the economic impact on the local population was spread more broadly. Finally, this solution required less investment for the organization.

- In one of the parks, they had created a separate camp with facilities for wildlife filming crews. This attracted some larger wildlife production teams and, in turn, created exposure for the park among a much wider audience. This was a low-cost way of attracting more visitors.

- In the remote locations of parks, connectivity is usually only available if a park invests in satellite connections. Some parks now have better connectivity than the capital of the country they are based in. Rather than using connectivity as a source of income, given the monopoly position of the park, they provide ample access, creating a constant flow of images and stories via social media, a very effective way of creating interests in a relevant target audience.

He followed up: 'A national park is just a stretch of land that has a certain designation attached to it, nothing else. There are no fences around the Masai Mara. The development of a piece of land in a successful national park comprises a set of steps that are mutually reinforcing'.

It starts with attractive fauna (and landscape). This drives all other aspects.

If the park has wildlife potential, investment in creating access is required, often by the government.

If the fauna and access provide an interesting combination, funds for facilities can be attracted, sometimes kick started by the park board itself, but more often by independent entrepreneurs.

The park and the facilities can attract visitors, who generate involvement with the park and the associated entrepreneurs.

This creates income for the staff, who are often local as well.

The personnel can protect the parks, leading to better and more interesting fauna.

The benefits for the local population increase the acceptance of the parks existence and further reduces pressure.

This circle reinforces itself, but the crucial component at the heart of the process is the richness of the wildlife experience, i.e. the landscape, the flora, and especially the fauna.

Like most businesses, a national park is influenced by the environment, economy, and society. However, parks are often located in remote areas with low population density and development. In these areas, the park is so large and significant in terms of economy and employment that it plays a major role in shaping the environmental, economic, and societal conditions in the surrounding region. Effective park management aims to strike a balance between the park's performance and the three key factors, by creating a platform that promotes ecological, economic, and societal development.

National parks as a design template for a platform company

Jack was taken aback by the similarities with his own thinking in the last few days. He concluded that the impact of being in nature aligns the thinking. After the lecture, Jack sought out Leopold to share some of his recent thoughts and reflect on the similarities.

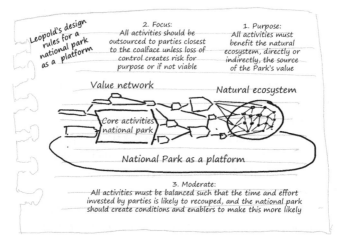

Figure 5.3: A national park, its ecosystem, and the design rules for the park as a platform.

He made a drawing with the natural ecosystem at its centre, being directly supported by the national park organization, and acting as a platform for other influences. The quality of this ecosystem determines the potential for development. Simply put, without it there would be no value to be generated at all. By supplying the ecosystem with the core facilities, value is created that enables the potential for growth. The growth is realized through a set of factors that are partly under direct control of the national park, partly facilitated or enabled by the national park, and partly outside the control of the national park.

Leopold explained how he was constantly choosing between three options of owning, facilitating, and leaving to the network. He had a few design rules:

1. The key purpose and source of value creation is the natural ecosystem. All activities that we promote through the platform must directly benefit the natural ecosystem or enable the support of these activities.
2. We then look at all different activities that are part of the national park that contribute directly or indirectly to the

continuing existence of the natural ecosystem. These include direct interference in nature, but also fundraising activities to finance the whole system.

All activities that can be executed by others should be executed by others, preferably by those closer to the animals, end customers, or local population, unless the loss of control impacts the quality of the natural ecosystem severely.

3. All activities must be balanced such that the money, time, and effort invested by parties and contributors result in a decent return, be it monetary or otherwise. The national parks organization should create a system of governance of the parks that makes this return more likely.

Typically, the realm of the national parks organization would include security, major infrastructure, access control, and wildlife management.

As Jack walked back to the tent with Caroline, he was anxious to superimpose the national park model onto his own situation.

He replaced the natural ecosystem with the end customers community, and the activities that they typically used M&S products for. This was the source of all the resources for the whole value chain. Without this group of end customers, the industry would cease to exist. If neglected, the end customers group would lose interest in the products and switch to a purely functional, price driven purchasing process, thus destroying much of their potential value.

Corollary 20: First priority for a player on a platform is the creation of value for the end user.

By defining the objective of the platform as creating value to the end customer community, Jack had also defined the arena in which M&S would focus its efforts. M&S was no longer a producer of goods, but a creator of value for that arena.

Design steps for a platform organization:

- Leopold's first rule focuses on preserving and growing the core source of value. All the activities of the firm, its partners, and even its end customers should be steered to maximize value for the end customer. This is very similar to the approach that Jack had defined for the channel conflict on the second day, i.e. focus on jointly creating more value so that customer euros are not spent outside your ecosystem.
- The second rule helps to build up a full list of stakeholders and contributors.
  - Many of these stakeholders generate their income directly from end customer spending.
  - Some stakeholders might generate value indirectly, for instance by creating traffic through M&S products, by building credibility, by providing a chance to improve skills, or to obtain insights into end customer preferences.
  - A third group of potential value contributors are the end customers themselves, as Jack had concluded the previous day.
- The three rules must ensure that the system is balanced and thus self-reinforcing. For each activity in the value chain, M&S should decide whether it would prefer to do it in-house or whether to partner on the platform. The design rules that Jack had found earlier that day would help him to make this decision:
  - Consider whether an activity in a more dynamic aspect of the value chain can be delegated to smaller, more nimble partners.
  - To attract the best partners, M&S has to ensure that these partners will benefit from joining, not just financially, but also by guaranteeing effective and efficient partners. M&S should look for opportunities to create lock-in. This should be the focus of the scale advantages of M&S.

How Coronara is structured as a platform

Jack's mind went back to the Coronara case he had discussed with the Agnellis the day before. Coronara had avoided direct cost competition in heart monitors by linking up with family doctors, making data available for direct interpretation and advice during a consultation.

He concluded that Coronara had turned itself into a platform, just as the national parks organization had.

As valuable as it is for a consumer to know his/her heart rate, it becomes much more valuable if it is linked to advice on how to interpret the results. Indeed, this is so valuable that this aspect of the experience was driving consumer preference and spend.

By linking the information from the monitor to the doctor, Coronara could provide that experience with its own machines. This had created a strong position, claiming a large portion of the money that people spend on improving their health.

Jack revisited the conversation that morning to determine underpinned the success. How was Coronara able to appropriate the value that was created in the network without overcharging and losing out to competitors? He now understood that all three aspects of the earlier game drive were in play:

- Efficiency: Coronara had built up a strong reputation in home-use heart monitors. It provided great support in terms of using the apparatus. A family doctor that joined the network would save time as Coronara took care of much of the customer interaction and support, as part of its customer service.
- Effectiveness: Because of the scale of the network, it contains a wide set of anonymous reference data that allow a family doctor to effectively compare measurements. Family doctors can also compare notes or ask for advice from fellow participants, a form of self-help that is greatly appreciated and cost effective.

– Lock-in: Once family doctors switched to Coronara they would build up an increasingly large set of patients that use the Coronara heart monitor to measure their health. If a family doctor wants to switch to another brand, they would lose all these patients, or have to issue them with a new monitor.

Having a leading value network did not mean that Coronara were complacent. On the contrary, they constantly ensured that their network was efficient, effective, and that it would not be beneficial to leave.

How different functions develop in a platform company

Jack reflected on M&S's position. The company would need to claim a role in the competitive value network. It was well-placed to do so as it had the largest set of end customers and professional users in the business. The M&S brand was well-known, which would make it easier for partners to create traction with a local enterprise, by tagging along on the recognition of the M&S brand.

But Jack still felt that they needed more to ensure the long-term future of the company.

Coronara's use of data was central to their strategy. M&S has data, in the form of client data, user data, profiles. Connected devices increasingly generate data on how the products are used. If the company could leverage this data and the data produced by its partners, it could greatly enhance the effectiveness of the value chain. He opened his mail to type a long reply to Falik.

So, what would the company look like if M&S follows these design rules? Jack collated the ideas that he had earlier developed for specific functions into a table.

Building a platform would require much more assertive management of M&S. Any flaw would quickly lead to loss of control or end customers. Jack though of his current control system that was based on the KPI framework that Falik had developed. This would be a great asset if it could be adjusted to measure the

	Classic	Platform
Branding	Create large brands that support dominant communication in public media	Promote viral growth Brands that grow peer-2-peer through the support of customers or fans
Sales	Create dominant position in point of sales and coordinated promotion	Develop a rich proposition over multiple channels with the aim to claim euros for the category
Innovation	Selection process to choose the right investment in high risk, high gain product innovations	Use customer base and position to attract innovation from loosely associated crowds of innovators
Supply	Standardize product or product components to achieve economies of scale	Personalized products where network and customers play a role in creating the value
Planning & strategy	Execute extensive research and forecasting on which business planning and control is based	Platform design, to strengthen the competitiveness of the value chain

Table 5.1 Differences in focus per function between classic and platform companies.

appropriate KPIs for platform optimization. Jack drafted some initial ideas in a second table:

Creating these tables had allowed Jack to gather his thoughts and zoom out to see the bigger picture. It seemed a logical step in the development of the corporate model.

At the start of industrialization, companies became competitive by being able to make stuff. Soon, large companies grew more advanced than the society surrounding them. A conglomerate with strongly integrated firms was more effective than the open market.

From the middle of the last century, markets developed, creating powerful new sources of innovation and growth. Companies returned to their core capabilities, outsourcing all other activities. Only those companies with an unhealthy level of control over their market can thrive in an integrated conglomerate.

	Classic	Platform
Brand:	Extra margin a company can charge because of brand	Value created in search, transaction, engagement and social traffic by engagement with the brand
Advertising	Number of people faced with message, the impact on recognition or attitude of the product/brand/firm	Amount of exchange between people, talking about the brand and people responding
Sales channels	Margin (% & €) on sales for a specific channel	Added value a customer is receiving through time saving in acquisition, effective acquisition and engagement. Results in Customer Lifetime Value
Market share:	Market share in market of similar products	Industry share of wallet of consumer spending
Innovation process:	Funnel process, I.e. The number & quality of ideas in each stage of the funnel	Share of innovative solutions around the industry that co-operate with the firm
Innovation	Sales of products less than a certain age, i.e. 2 years	Value generated by innovation on top of core products sales.
Supply chain:	Cost to produce a specific item	Cost for the whole value chain to deliver the full experience and personalization to the end customer

Table 5.2: Differences in key metrics/objectives between classic and platform companies in some key functions.

Today, even core competencies are not the safe haven they once were, and companies must now confront the next wave: after integration and core competencies they must manage their ecosystem. By managing the value network, they can create a submarket in the economy that is more effective and/or efficient than others attracting revenue and specific value.

M&S must embrace this trend and become a platform company.

Corollary 21: The platform company is a natural next step in the evolution of the dominant company model: From integrated firm to conglomerate to start-up to platform company.

Jack realized that there was a heck of a lot of work to be done. Yet, he was convinced that this was the only way forward. Only by creating a platform could M&S ensure a microcosmos in which its capabilities as an integrated corporation could be leveraged. It was the only way for M&S to withstand the onslaught of the crowd. Jack could do this by making all aspects of the industry part of his internal management scope.

He should have a plan ready in time for the end of year board meeting in order to ensure support for the drastic changes he was proposing. He fired off an email to Alice, the head of strategy & planning.

Subject: Strategy process for a platform company

Hi Alice,

During my trip, I have had time to process the strategy update you sent me last month. While I agree on the analysis, I differ on the solution.

We face several existential threats, e.g. retailers sourcing directly from China, fast-growing newcomers claiming lower price points with more attractive brands, diminishing return on our marketing campaigns, innovations that take place outside our control, even outside our industry, customers becoming less loyal, e-commerce bypassing our existing sales channels.

I think these trends will only strengthen due to further growth of globalization and digitalization. Consequently, the business environment is a more dynamic, less predictable space, where smaller, nimbler players can gain an advantage over large integrated firms such as M&S.

I do not believe we should follow these trends by behaving more like a startup, or local small firms. Though there is nothing wrong with becoming more agile and nimble, we will never be able to beat the host of new firms in our industry at their own game by copying them.

For instance, by moving downstream to create local distribution presence and a direct personalization service for end customers, we make ourselves more vulnerable to local firms while simultaneously losing some of our scale and cost advantages.

Instead, I think we should address the challenge with a different paradigm. We should build a network of partners that is nimble, responsive, and local. This allows us to beat off this new threat, in marketing, in sales & distribution, in innovation, and in production.

By supporting such a network, we can ensure that it creates more value than other channels in the industry, or even other ways for customers to spend their euros.

By facilitating our partners, we can make them more efficient and effective, ensuring that they benefit from staying within our value network.

We should transform M&S to become a platform company that supports and moderates this value network.

Yesterday, I asked Falik to create a value network analysis; maybe you can reach out to him and collaborate on this. It should include not just the activities within our company, but also all activities that create value for the end customer based on our products.

More specifically, I would like to ask you to assess each activity and each entity on three aspects:

- *How much value is created for the end customer?*
- *Can we leave the activities to the ecosystem, or would this harm our ability to maximize value creation?*
- *Can we facilitate others to create value, by leveraging our product, our network, our client base, innovations in the market, or any other means?*

What I would like you to do is to investigate how we can use data that we collect throughout the value network to optimize performance. A starting point might be a way to better predict demand based on activities in the network. You should also consider data that contributes to the performance of our partners.

I suspect that we do not have much of the data we need at this stage. Perhaps you can estimate the work that would be involved in going through the whole network and make a draft capacity plan. I would like to ensure that the plan is ready for the board meeting at the end of the year. That means that I have to discuss it with board members in October.

Kind regards, Jack

Introduction Chapter 6: How do I lead the transformation?

As he pushed the send button, Jack realized that, by now, he must have propelled the whole company into a state of confusion. As he looked back at his notes, he started to realize the enormity of the disruption they were facing, as well as the changes that M&S would need to make to respond to his plans. This would require more than 'rearranging the chairs on the deck of the Titanic.' He needed to change the context in which the company was operating. He also realized that it was just not possible to take control of all reins now , not least because it would go against the context and culture he was trying to create. As this dilemma bounced around his brains, Jack poured himself a whisky and joined Caroline in the seating area in front of the tent.

6.   Leading through purpose: Defining the core value that your organization is meant to produce

Monkeys on guard – A sustainable contribution to a company's purpose should determine organizational design

When Jack and Caroline woke, it was cloudy, and so they had a relaxed morning. He browsed through the pages of the *Selfish Gene* and was touched, as usual, by the strength of the analytical paradigm explaining nature through natural gene selection.

The book does not focus on species or individuals, but rather on 'genotypes', the specific genes that drive the shape, form, and behavior of individuals and species. These traits, in turn, determine survival rate. The animals and plants are just vehicles, 'phenotypes' that ensure the prolongation of the gene's life; not because the gene wants to survive, but as a logical consequence of the fact that any genes that do not ensure propagation simply disappear, leaving those that do.

Jack and Caroline left the camp for a game drive at 8am, heading toward a bend in the river, where there was a small, light forest of fever trees. The beautiful yellow trees were home to a group of monkeys that were very excited, which suggested that there might be a predator around. The vehicle stopped and they scanned the branches of the trees, one by one, with binoculars. It took some time, but finally they spotted the source of all the excitement, a leopard resting on a branch of one of the trees. It was so close that it was a surprise that they had not spotted it immediately. Jack was struck by the leopard's ability to blend into the background.

Not far away from the leopard was a particularly loud juvenile monkey, continuously raising alarm calls. Why was this monkey staying so close to the leopard, risking life and limb by shouting and drawing attention to itself? Surely, the group  benefitted from his watchtower function? But it seemed that such behavior would reduce the chance of the shouty youngster surviving. Other monkeys were busy finding a safe hiding place, high up in the trees. Surely, this strategy made more sense?

If the monkeys were to be split into two groups, a shouting group and a hiding group, in due course, because of the difference in survival rate, the shouting trait would disappear.

'The monkeys must be close relatives,' Jack decided. A gene can persist by ensuring the survival of the individual it is in, or by ensuring that individuals that are likely to have the same gene survive, i.e. close relatives. Even if the shouting reduced the chances of the individual juvenile, it increased the prospect of the survival of his brothers and sisters, who would carry the same gene in 50 per cent of the cases. Thus, a gene that causes some individuals to shout can ensure a higher overall survival rate in animals that live in family groups.

They spend some time observing the leopard, until it swiftly climbed backwards down along the trunk, and disappeared into the riverbed.

Raison d'être or purpose, the meme that a company is coded to promulgate

After a light breakfast, they returned to the tent and Jack opened his laptop. He had seen many references in consultant's presentations on evolution, survival of the fittest, and Darwin, suggesting that it was not the biggest but the most adaptable firms that survive. Based on what he had observed that morning, Jack concluded that the reality was much more subtle and complex.

Following his line of thought from the evening before, he decided to confront the current disruption and the required response as existential for the survival of M&S. 'What exactly constitutes the survival of a firm? Its brand? Its product? Employment for its workforce? Its capital?'

If it was capital, why are so many firms shredding capital by buying back shares? Surely, capital can exist outside firms. Capital was more akin to energy or proteins.

Many firms have failed because they lacked sufficient product innovation, so surely the consistent availability of products cannot be equated to firm survival.

Some companies were quite successful, buying new selling brands all the time, especially in fast-moving consumer goods (FMCG), so brand survival does not equate to company survival.

So, many of the obvious aspects of firms, which are discussed a lot, do not seem to be the essence of a firm. Maybe he should view the company with its capital, brands, and products, as a phenotype of something more profound, which drives the traits of the firm, just like a gene drives the traits of an individual. 'What drives the shape of a firm?', Jack pondered, 'other than external circumstances, such as competition or market developments.'

He tried to identify the essence of his family firm: its values, its practices, and its leadership style. Maybe these are the genes Jack was searching for, a sort of mental gene, 'Memes' as Dawkins calls them. To Jack, the M&S memes are about the way they did business, the management practices that have shaped M&S over the decades.

In M&S's case, the essence of the company is about continuously updating and adapting the way things work with new management insights.

Jack drafted a list of principles that could work and marked the one that he believed was most applicable to M&S. Jack recalled how his predecessors had embraced Taylorism, but had also adopted sociotechnology. His uncle was a proud American, but he had also travelled to Japan to learn from the source. Based on this, Jack decided that the M&S core meme was the ability to implement new ways of operating.

Example Memes,

What do the management principles and habits of a firm code for

* Most creative solution or design
* Most effective in integration
* Most frugal in executing
* Most widely used
* Highest level of comfort
* Most effective executor of new management ideas ◀——— M & S
* Most reliable solution
* Least impact on environment
* Etc.

Table 6.1: Example memes that express the way a company works.

The key to M&S's success is its ability to understand what better methods of organization are being developed and then implement these new methods quickly and effectively.

If M&S could not sustain these values, it might lose its purpose, and, consequently, its capital, staff, and brand might just as well be employed somewhere else.

Jack was increasingly convinced by this idea. He could determine the company's future by focusing on sustaining the essence of the firm. This felt much closer to what he believed than the conventional five-year approach to planning for the future, which relied on many assumptions in a business environment that was becoming increasingly fluid.

The business-meme paradigm, freed Jack to approach M&S strategy in a more self-adapting way. The strategy question shifts from: 'What plan do we need to put in place for the coming five years to be successful and outsmart competition?' to 'What management principles need to prevail, to ensure that our company best responds to challenges and changes in the environment?'

At this level, the company becomes a platform for the promulgation of the best management principles, of business memes, either inside or outside the legal entity that is the firm.

The objective is not to own or control everything. The objective is to create a value network in which the desired business memes can flourish sustainably.

Switching to the platform paradigm unleashes the company from the shackles of process design, ISO9000, integrated enterprise resource planning (ERPs), Prince project management practices, and other process-oriented, high overhead ways of trying to optimize a business.

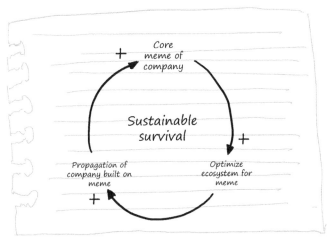

Figure 6.1: The survival of the purpose of a firm is based on its meme or its purpose, and by promoting the ecosystem that increases the chances of success.

The focus of the platform paradigm is much more systemic, and the benefits greater but much more indirect. It benefits from reality focused techniques, such as lean, scrum, and agile startup.

This paradigm greatly simplifies the explanation of the success of, say, Google or e-commerce, and it pinpoints why many large firms are unable to create a sustainable business.

Jack decided that the M&S company meme will be: 'M&S is best in executing new ideas or ways of working, quickly, effectively, and on a large scale.'

Tea at the tent: Survival should be defined as survival of purpose, not revenue or capital

As Jack's latest ideas slowly sank in, he looked up from his laptop and scanned the bush in front of the tent. 'Here is a great idea,' he said to Caroline, as she put away her book and ordered some coffee.

'I want to redefine the purpose of the firm. Currently, it is about the value of future cash flow, but this has driven us to the situation we are in now, lacking the ability to control our performance or our destiny in a society that is becoming increasingly fluent. I have come up with a purpose that is much closer to my heart, and much more suitable to respond to future challenges: Our company is a platform whose objective is to maximize the survival rate of the core values and management practices that we find important at M&S, and that ensure our future survival'.

He filled Caroline in on the background behind his thinking, and she quickly grasped the concept and started to add to it. They talked about many of the sights they had seen that week in the park and drew comparisons with the gene survival vs meme survival paradigm.

'Another way of looking at it, is through history,' Caroline added. 'Take the ancient Greeks. At the time of the wars between Athens and Sparta the objective of the competition could be defined at two levels: Who would conquer the other's land or whose ideas would become dominant? History tends to focus on the first question when it comes to war and battles, on who is in command. But the second question is much more interesting and produces problems that have much greater impact on the lives of the people concerned.

If Sparta is an individual state shaped by memes that code for battle readiness and war, then Athens is a state shaped by memes coding for democracy and great thinking. The history of this competitive battle can be evaluated in two ways:

- At individual state level: the Spartans overcame the Athenians through military power. This was only temporary as decades later

they, in turn, were annihilated first by the Macedonians, then by the Romans.
- At a meme level: the battle continues, but we have seen a systematic growth of democracy at the cost of military regimes. Historically, the Athenian memes have gained the upper ground.

If both aspects of Greek society could be monetized, which one would you want to invest in: land to create harvest or ideas that create a pleasant life? Would you rather own a piece of land that is vulnerable to being conquered by the Macedonians? Or would you prefer to own ideas on philosophy and democracy that are the core of Western values and societies? In other words, would you rather live in a society that is run by outsiders, but who share your ideas, or in a society that is run by insiders but that comes up with ideas that you despise? Which is the more valuable option?

For your business, we could compare value with the ability to contribute to the quality of human existence. The management practices that drive the ability to create this value will be the genes of a company.

How the Platform Company creates new leadership challenges

As was so often the case, Caroline was way ahead of him. The history of Athens and Sparta supported his thinking on memes. More importantly, it prompted a more personal question: what kind of company did he want to pass on to the next generations? And how was he going to lead the company to that future?

Even though Jack had inherited his position in the firm, he was very conscious that this did not mean that people would simply accept his leadership.

In fact, he had consciously worked on developing a leadership style that chimed with this beliefs as well as being accepted within the firm. Although Jack's nature was to trust people and manage through objectives, he had learned that some level of directive leadership greatly improved performance and acceptance. It was also a way of mediating any ambiguity on objectives, and offered people a familiar ritual that afforded a sense of structure and security. Furthermore, he had a strong sense that he should behave as he expected his team should behave, not just for moral reasons, but also because, as the leader, he should set an example.

As Jack shifted M&S towards becoming a platform company, he realized that there were three further challenges to his leadership style:

1. The role of the firm must extend to the whole value network, greatly expanding the scope of subjects to manage.
2. In those aspects where the firm plays a role within its platform, the firm must work with partners or end customers who do not accept M&S as an authority. In these situations, his leadership can only be indirect.
3. The boundaries between internal and external will become more ambiguous.

As an ecosystem around a platform company, the process of value creation is much more autonomous. Jack listed the three key principles that he believed would help him lead the transformation.

1. Strengthen the focus on delivering value to the end customer as the source of money in the ecosystem.
2. Organize the platform to ensure that parties optimize their value creation. This ensures that it will win against other ecosystems, other places for the end customer to spend their euros.
3. Jack made M&S's core meme the third, crucial ingredient: 'the most effective execution of new ideas.' This has to be the guiding principle that M&S enshrines in the platform it's building.

After lunch, there were a few hours to spare before travelling back to Nairobi, and Jack decided to share some of his thoughts and plans with the team.

Subject: Redefining M&S as a platform company

As many of you will have noticed, the trip to Africa has given me an opportunity to take some distance from the day-to-day operational issues and think about the future.

We are confronting a lot of undesired developments in our business at the moment, for example:

1 We are losing position in the market to upstarts that create considerable exposure and sales at very low cost.
2 Big retail clients are squeezing our margins, or threatening to go direct, whilst going direct via e-commerce carries the risk of a price war.
3 The most impactful innovation is increasingly happening outside our company, outside our control, and even outside our industry.
4 Small local suppliers are harvesting the most interesting business, pushing us toward the role of a commodity supplier.

The last few years we have been trying to cope with these disruptions by doubling down on what we have always done. I thank you all for your great drive and dedication, even if this has not turned the tide. I have concluded that if we continue to follow this route the position of M&S will, inevitably, deteriorate and will no longer be in line with our proud heritage.

It is clear to me that the current developments are even more profound and that our response should therefore be to confront this new reality more honestly. The success of our firm depends on our ability to become part of this new reality.

We need to embrace all aspects of what contributes to value for our end customers, the value creation network, which includes suppliers, resellers, end customers, service providers, and any other partners.

We must immerse ourselves in the whole value creation network and drive its improvement, even if other parties or end customers are in the lead.

We need to become the prime platform on which the parties in the value creation network operate. This includes:

- *Facilitating brand building between end customers online*
- *Enabling value added shopping experiences for our resellers*
- *Enlisting innovators to scale up via our client base*
- *Empowering and facilitating local firms to create added value around our products*

I would summarize these steps, as: 'We need to become a platform company'.

To behave like a platform company externally means that we must behave as such internally. The journey ahead is so unpredictable, so dynamic, and so fast that we cannot rely on a top-down plan alone to execute this transformation. Instead, I would like to invite each of you to join in.

I am asking you to focus on those aspects of your work that contribute to end customer value. In return, I will commit to enabling you to accelerate anything that contributes.

Earlier this week, I began addressing some of the changes that I think fit with this approach. I would like to invite you next Tuesday to block out your agenda and start working on making the platform company a reality in our firm.

Regards, Jack

Leaving for home

As Jack closed his laptop, he felt a sense of both relief and exuberance. He felt better than had for many years. Even though he could not wait to get started next Monday, he turned his attention to his surroundings. The African savannah had brought him so much insight and inspiration. He was deeply grateful. He looked up at Caroline and they walked together to the other side of the camp to have a last look at the waterhole.

They observed the beauty in silence as they saw a shy and enigmatic antelope carefully approach the water. It was medium-sized, and dark brown with white markings.

As they were preparing to leave, Africa bade them farewell through a Bushbuck, a beautiful animal, drinking water, frequently stopping to scan the surroundings and then trotting back into the bush, becoming completely invisible as soon as it was engulfed by the foliage.

ack had the animal imprinted on his mind as they walked back to the tent, as they were driven to the airstrip by Mike, and as they climbed on board. It was only when the airplane took off that Jack found the spell of the African plains broken. As they approached Nairobi, he said to Caroline sitting next to him:

'Even if this was a short trip, I am excited to get home and get cracking at the profusion of inspirational ideas that the Masai Mara has given me. It shows once again that we cannot beat nature for its depth of insights. It also shows that Suzi were right to press ahead with this trip, switching from just working harder and doing more of the same to thinking deeper and doing smarter things'.

Background & Acknowledgements

This book was written over a period of several years but is the cumulation of over thirty years of experience. It is a contribution to the thinking that is required to shape the world that the next generation, including my own children, are set to inherit. Not just the state of affairs, but also the ability to actively engage with it based on up-to-date thinking and approaches.

Below I have listed some key experiences, books, and people that have contributed to the development of my ideas and the realization of the book. This is meant to both acknowledge the contributors and give the reader some insight into the sources behind 'The Platform Company'.

- 1985: Tuition on systems theory, by Professor Jan in't Veld at Technical University Delft, Department of Mechanical engineering.
- 1989: Master's in Systems Modeling, with Professor Okko Bosgra, at Technical University Delft, Faculty of Control Engineering.
- 1992: Introduction to the book The Goal (and its successors) by Eliyahu M. Goldratt, which sharpened my thinking through the theory of constraints, and which later inspired me to write The Platform Company as a narrative.
- 1993: Tuition on business process analysis, as well as many other concepts that have helped me make sense of business, by IMD professors Tom Vollmann, Per Jenster, and their colleagues, as part of Unilever Technical Management Program for high-potential trainees.
- 1994: Reading The Selfish Gene by Richard Dawkins, which helped me to make sense of nature, especially during my many trips to Africa.

- 1995: Building a factory in the UK for a 'smart' medical device, and the coaching I received from Frank de Fouw, a true master of project management.
- 1996: Introduction to The Key to Strategy is Context by Stanley M Davies, a paper that gave me crucial insight into the essence of strategy execution.
- 1998: Training in Japan on Total Productive Maintance (lean production) by JIPM, strengthening my strong conviction in the value of empowerment.
- 1999: Experience of turning around an ice cream factory together with JIPM, and the coaching I received from José Cavanna, which taught me the value of gemba.
- 2002: Joining Adnovate, a startup, and later scaleup, well ahead of its time, building a platform company for automating marketing processes. A single instance, Software-as-a-Service solution from the start.
- 2011: Introduction to The Lean Machine by Dantar Oosterwal, who demonstrates how chasing a specific improvement sets you up to lose control of your destiny.
- 2014: Working on publication of digital transformation articles with Eric Campinini in Paris and the Bearingpoint digital team in Amsterdam. This started my interest in writing a book.
- 2015: Tuition at Yale University on the Threadless case – a company that is a true example of creating many kinds of value for its stakeholders in addition to money – by Prof. J. Nalebuff, the author of The Art of Strategy: A Game Theorist's Guide to Success in Business and Life.
- 2015: Organizing round tables with Prof. Frambach to test business model ideas on representatives from industry and business.
  Further down the path: Prof. Frambach has spent many hours discussing and reviewing The Platform Company.
- 2016: Organizing my initial thoughts on a potential publication with Natalya Permyakova, a sharp, driven, and helpful colleague at Bearingpoint.

- 2019: Visiting Nairobi and Kajiado to investigate how a more regular water supply could change the lives of communities and working with my colleagues at MegaGroup and Better Future on a design for a new business model to achieve this; the start of Waterstarters.
- 2020: Allard Winterink helps me navigate the world of publishing.
- 2021: Philosophizing with Tjardus van Citters, whose publication efforts have inspired my own, and always asking the question: 'what will you start doing when you ~~grow up~~ get serious about what you really want in life?'.

These are all significant steps along my path to *The Platform Company*, but, above all, the book would not have existed if Marie-Anne, my wife and the love of my life, and I had not decided, thirty years ago, to jointly wander through the African wilderness, in much less luxurious conditions than Jack and Caroline. The African plains that have given us such a connection and understanding of nature have continued to inspire us throughout our lives.

Further reading

The books and articles that have inspired me during my career, and which I have used to develop this book, can be a good source if you want to deepen your understanding of a specific subject addressed in this book. Each source has a short comment on what it can bring to the reader in the context of this book.

Chapter 1: Branding & Marcom

Branding & peer-to-peer

Edelman, David C. (2010). "Branding in the Digital Age: You're Spending Your Money in All the Wrong Places", *Harvard Business Review*, Cambridge, MA, December issue.
Suggest focusing on the customer decision journey and on marketing spend at the right spot.

Holt, Douglas (2016). "Branding in the Age of Social Media", *Harvard Business Review*, Cambridge, MA, March issue.
Introduces Crowd Cultures as a concept to more effectively manage performance of branding in social media.

Kumar, V., Petersen, J. Andrew, and Robert P. Leone (2007). "How Valuable Is Word of Mouth?", *Harvard Business Review*, Cambridge, MA, October issue.
A method for identifying customer value based on their referral value (marketing) rather than just on their current purchases

Laurenson, Lydia (2015). "Don't Try to Be a Publisher and a Platform at the Same Time", *Harvard Business Review*, Cambridge, MA, January issue.
Addresses the choice a platform owner needs to make: Will you go for scale or for editorial quality? You can't have them both.

Piskorski, Mikołaj Jan (2011). "Social Strategies that Work", *Harvard Business Review*, Cambridge, MA, November issue.
Addresses the idea that success on social platforms requires people-to-people connection.

Rose, John (2012). *The Value of Our Digital Identity*, Boston Consulting Group, Liberty Global, Inc. November 2011, http://www.libertyglobal.com/PDF/public-policy/The-Value-of-Our-Digital-Identity.pdf 2017
Analyses the phenomenon of digital identity and how its value can be assessed for consumers as well as organizations.

Impact of trust and (lack of) transparency

The Economist (2001). "The Lemon Dilemma".
  http://www.economist.com/node/813705
  Summary of the article "The Market for Lemons" on the influence of uncertainty (lack of trust) in market mechanisms.

Loch, Christoph, Sting, Fabian J., Huchzermeier, Arnd, and Christiane Decker (2012). "Finding Profit in Fairness (Team Bank)", *Harvard Business Review*, Cambridge, MA, September issue.
  Case of a bank that by instilling transparency and fairness in the way it operates grows rapidly in a crowded banking industry.

Miller, Geoffrey (2009). *Sex, Status and the Evolution of Consumerism.* New York: Viking.
  Explores human (consumer) behavior through evolutionary psychology.

Zahavi, Amotz (1997). *The Handicap Principle: A Missing Piece of Darwin's Puzzle.* Oxford: Oxford University Press.
  A great and accessible piece of ecological analysis that helps to explain animal design as well as human behavior.

Micro-segmentation

Harrington, Richard J., and Anthony K. Tjan (2008). "Transforming Strategy One Customer at a Time", *Harvard Business Review*, Cambridge, MA, March issue.
  Developing a transformational strategy by diving into the end user and building a new proposition one group at a time.

Oliver, Keith, Moeller, Leslie H., and Bill Lakenanr (2012). "Smart Customization: Profitable Growth Through Tailored Business Streams, Strategy + Business (Booz Allen now PWC, New York)".
  https://www.strategy-business.com/article/04104?gko=951a6
  Suggests that standardization is not the best route to profit. Instead, companies should focus on identifying specific segments and delivering the right level of customization.

Chapter 2: Sales & distribution

Customer experience

Avery, Jill, Fournier, Susan, and John Wittenbraker (2016). "Unlock the Mysteries of Your Customer Relationships", *Harvard Business Review*, Cambridge, MA, July–August issue.
  Understanding how customer relations can be improved by using data beyond demographics.

Edelman, David C., and Marc Singer (2015). "Competing on Customer Journeys", *Harvard Business Review*, Cambridge, MA, November issue.

How to make customer journeys so compelling that customers follow your lead and stay with you.

Gulati, Ranjay (2007). "Silo Busting: How to Execute on the Promise of Customer Focus", *Harvard Business Review*, Cambridge, MA, May issue.
Discusses managing the customer experience over internal silos and the importance of customer focus.

Neslin, Scott A., Grewal, Dhruv, Leghorn, Robert et al. (2006). "Challenges and Opportunities in Multichannel Customer Management", *Journal of Service Research*, Volume 9, No. 2, November. [page extension?]
Good overview of multi-channel customer management challenges, including evaluating resource allocation, coordination, and channel conflicts.

Value creation beyond the product

Ander, Willard N., and Neil Z. Stern (2004). *Winning at Retail: Developing Sustained Models for Retail Success*, Hoboken, NY: John Wiley & Sons.
A great introduction to key differentiators in retail.

Fawkes, Piers (2011). *Future of Retail*, New York: PSFK.
In-depth report on trends in retail (not for those with a tiny wallet).

Kauffeld, Rich, Sauer, Johan, and Sara Bergson (2009). "Partners at the Point of Sale, Strategy + Business (Booz Allen, now PWC, New York)".
https://www.strategy-business.com/article/07305?gko=a8f7c.

Mikitani, Hiroshi (2013). "Rakuten's CEO on Humanizing E-Commerce", *Harvard Business Review*, Cambridge, MA, November issue,
Discusses the role of social and personal experience in e-commerce.

Sorescu, Alina, Frambach, Ruud T., Jagdip Singh et al. (2016). "Innovation in Retail Business Models", *Journal of Retailing*, , 87S (1, 2011) S3–S16
An extremely valuable analysis of how to structure value creation and value appropriation in retail business models.

Browsing behavior

Avery, Jill, Steenburgh, Thomas J., Deighton, John, and Mary Caravella (2012). "Adding Bricks to Clicks: Predicting the Patterns of Cross-Channel Elasticities Over Time", *Journal of Marketing*, Vol. 76, No. 3, pp. 96-111.
Examines the impact of adding new channels to existing ones.

Prins, Herbert H.T. (1996). *Ecology and Behaviour of the African Buffalo: Social Inequality and Decision-Making*, London: Chapman & Hall.
A surprising story of how advanced social behavior can develop in a buffalo herd.

Stearns, Stephen C. (2009). "Principles of Evolution, Ecology and Behavior: Lecture 32 – Economic Decisions for the Foraging Individual", New Haven, CT: Open Yale Courses.
http://oyc.yale.edu/ecology-and-evolutionary-biology/eeb-122/lecture-32
Part of a lecture series that is a comprehensive introduction to evolutionary biology.

Game theory

Dixit, Avinash K., and Barry J. Nalebuff (1993). *The Art of Strategy: A Game Theorist's Guide to Success in Business and Life*, New York: Norton & Company
Clear, concise, and not shy of in-depth analysis. This book is a great way to understand Game theory and its application in business.

The Economist (2016). "Game Theory Prison Breakthrough".
https://www.economist.com/news/economics-brief/21705308-fifth-our-series-seminal-economic-ideas-looks-nash-equilibrium-prison
Introduction to the Nash Equilibrium and its impact on economic research

Erhun, Feryal, and Pınar Keskinocak (2003). *Game Theory in Business Applications*, Stanford, CA: Stanford University Press.
Introduction to game theory in business.

McNamara, John M., and Franz J. Weissing (2010). *Evolutionary Game Theory*, Cambridge: Cambridge University Press.
http://www.rug.nl/research/gelifes/tres/publications/_pdf/socialbehavch4.pdf
Examines the way game theory can be applied in ecological processes, such as mate selection.

Chapter 3: Innovation

Innovation management

Anthony, Scott D. (2012). "The New Corporate Garage", *Harvard Business Review*, Cambridge, MA, September issue.
Inspiring article on how best-practice innovation for large companies has developed from lone inventors, corporate labs, and venture-capital-backed startups to corporate catalysts.

Bonabeau, Eric, Bodick, Neil, and Robert W. Armstrong (2008). "A More Rational Approach to New-Product Development", *Harvard Business Review*, Cambridge, MA, March issue.
Creates a clear distinction between early and late stage of product development, e.g. between startup and scaleup.

Gertner, Jon (2012). *The Idea Factory: Bell Labs and the Great Age of American Innovation*, New York: Penguin Press.
To understand the origin of large R&D facilities this book gives a hugely interesting history of one of the greatest of them all, the lab that gave us transistors, IC and Cell phones.

Hansen, Morten T., and Julian Birkinshaw (2007). "The Innovation Value Chain", *Harvard Business Review*, Cambridge, MA, June issue.
Describes classic innovation funnel management approach.

Oosterwal, Dantar P. (2010). *The Lean Machine: How Harley Davidson Drove Top-Line Growth and Profitability with Revolutionary Lean Product Development*, New York: AMACOM.

Bringing Lean to innovation is not just about efficiency and funnel management. By ensuring you learn from development, speed of innovation is increased.

Thomke, Stefan, and Donald Reinertsen (2012). "Six Myths Of Product Development: The Fallacies that Cause Delays, Undermine Quality, and Raise Costs", *Harvard Business Review*, Cambridge, MA, May issue.
Shows how innovation processes can be flawed, especially if based on 'old' Taylor-based approach.

Open / digital innovation

Blank, Steve (2013). "Why the Lean Startup Changes Everything", *Harvard Business Review*, Cambridge, MA, May issue.
Discusses the power of starting business with minimal overheads and preparation, through focus and short feedback cycles.

Chesbrough, Henry W. (2006). *Open Innovation: The New Imperative for Creating and Profiting from Technology*, Cambridge, MA: Harvard Business School Press.
A classic for understanding open innovation. It focuses on sharing, co-creation, and the early stage of innovation.

Hippel, Eric von (2005). *Democratizing Innovation*, Cambridge, MA: MIT Press.
Studies the way innovation moves to the end users, and how corporations can adapt to this trend.

Porter, Michael E., and James E. Heppelmann (2015). "How Smart, Connected Products are Transforming Companies", *Harvard Business Review*, Cambridge, MA, October issue.
Addresses strategic question that are emerging with the growth of IoT products.

Tatikonda, Mohan V., and Stephen R. Rosenthal (2000). "Successful Execution of Product Development Projects: Balancing Firmness and Flexibility in the Innovation Process", *Journal of Operations Management*,18 (2000): pp. 401-425.
Suggests that a higher success rate in product development is linked to firmness in objectives and evaluation combined with flexibility in project management autonomy and resource allocation.

Chapter 4: Supply chain

Supply chain management

Kuipers H., and P. van Amelsvoort (1990). *Slagvaardig organiseren. Inleiding in de sociotechniek als integrale ontwerpleer*, Deventer: Kluwer.
An introduction to how self-organizing teams can outperform Taylorian organization (Dutch).

Vollmann, Thomas E., Berry, William L., and Clay D. Whybark (1984). *Manufacturing Planning and Control Systems* (3rd edn), Chicago: Irwin Inc.
A classic source for understanding manufacturing logistics and planning.

Womack, James P., Jones, Daniel T., and Daniel Roos (1990). *The Machine that Changed the World*, New York: Macmillan.

An accessible introduction to the concepts of lean, especially the way it transformed, first, the Japanese manufacturing industry.

Value creation network

Author? (2011). "Technology and Society: The 'Maker' Movement Could Change How Science is Taught and Boost Innovation: It May Even Herald a New Industrial Revolution", *Economist Quarterly*, Q4 2011.
Discusses the coming of age of the maker movement in society and business.
The Economist (2010). "The Wiki Way", 25 September.
Discussion on the role that internet can play in business and society through crowds sourcing.
Evans, Philip, and Bob Wolf (2005). "Collaboration Rules", *Harvard Business Review*, Cambridge, MA, July–August issue.
Collaboration can be enhanced through the development of the right environment, an environment that produces cheap plentiful transactions.
Heimans, Jeremy, and Henry Timms (2014). "Understanding 'New Power'", *Harvard Business Review*, Cambridge, MA, December issue.
Analyses the shift of power from traditional industries toward new digital players.
Keiningham, Timothy L., Aksoy, Lerzan, Buoye, Alexander, and Bruce Cooil (2011). "Customer Loyalty Isn't Enough: Grow Your Share of Wallet", *Harvard Business Review*, Cambridge, MA, October issue.
Addresses the issue that to properly guide value it is essential to evaluate from a customer perspective.
Malone, Thomas W., Laubacher, Robert, and Tammy Johns (2011). "The Age of Hyper Specialization", *Harvard Business Review*, Cambridge, MA, July–August issue.
How jobs become so specialized that they can be mixed and matched, also from the cloud
Mesquita, Luiz F., Anand, Jaideep, and Thomas H. Brush (2008). "Comparing the Resource-Based and Relation Views: Knowledge Transfer and Spillover in Vertical Alliances", *Strategic Management Journal*, Vol. 29, No. 9 (September): pp 913-941.
Finds that the true source of competitive advantage in vertical alliances is determined by relational performance, based on survey of 253 suppliers to the equipment industry.
Womack, James P., and Daniel T. Jones (2005). "Lean Consumption", *Harvard Business Review*, Cambridge, MA, March issue.
Companies can reap huge benefits by delivering customers time and effort, and by delivering exactly what they want, where and when they want it.

Chapter 5: Platform strategy

Competitive strategy

Collins, Jim C. (2001). *Good to Great: Why Some Companies Make the Leap and Others Don't*, New York: Harper Collins.

The book establishes common characteristics of successful companies, suggesting that this is a recipe for success. After so many years it proved the reverse, as it turned out that these recipes are not good predictors of survival, indeed, many of the great companies studied have since failed.

Mauboussin, Michael J. (2012). "The True Measures of Success", *Harvard Business Review*, Cambridge, MA, October issue.

How to avoid using output measurements as a prediction for future success.

Porter, Michael E., and James E. Heppelmann (1980). *Competitive Strategy: Techniques for Analyzing Industries and Competitors*, New York: Free Press.

An evergreen in strategy. Even though digitalization was not eminent at the time of writing, its analysis regarding fragmenting industries gives very useful insights into what is happening in business at the moment.

Stalk, George Jr., Evans, Philip, and Lawrence E. Shulman (1992). "Competing on Capabilities: The New Rules of Corporate Strategy", *Harvard Business Review*, Cambridge, MA, March–April issue.

Classic introduction into the capability focused development of strategy

Zook, Chris (2007). "Finding Your Next Core Business", *Harvard Business Review*, Cambridge, MA, April issue.

Systematic approach to finding new core activities that drive the future of your business.

Digital and ecosystem dynamics

Barfield, Thomas J. (1989). *The Perilous Frontier: Nomadic Empires and China, 221 BC to AD 1757*, Cambridge: Blackwheel Publishers.

A brilliant and inspiring book that analyses the underlying dynamics of China with its nomadic neighbors. The author finds that it is not the accidental genius of leaders, or the lack of them, that drive history, but that events can be explained by a typical sequence of events, or instability that has occurred several times in similar form.

Hagel, John III, Seely Brown, John, and Lang Davison (2008). "Shaping Strategy in a World of Constant Disruption", *Harvard Business Review*, Cambridge, MA, October issue.

Addresses design principles for a platform business ecosystem

Ismael, Salim, Makone, Michael S., and Yuri van Geest (2014). *Exponential Organizations: Why New Organizations are Ten Times Better, Faster, and Cheaper than Yours (and What To Do About It)*, New York: Diversion Books.

Describes how the current digitalized business ecosystem allows companies to grow exponentially.

Lansiti, Marco, and Roy Levien (2004). "Strategy as Ecology", *Harvard Business Review*, Cambridge, MA, March issue.

Discusses several cases of companies that optimized their ecosystem rather than the internal organization using simple frameworks.

McWaters, R. Jesse (2015). "The Future of Financial Services: How Disruptive Innovations are Reshaping the Way Financial Services are Structured, Provisioned
and Consumed". World Economic Forum, Cologne, June 2015.

A broad study of the impact of digitalization on particularly susceptible industry.
Key findings on platforms (p.13).Lansiti, Marco, and Roy Levien (2004). "Strategy
as Ecology", Harvard Business Review, Cambridge, MA, March issue.
Discusses several cases of companies that optimized their ecosystem rather than
the internal organization using simple frameworks.

Business model innovation

Amit, Raphael, and Christoph Zott (2012). "Creating Value Through Business Model
Innovation", *MIT Sloan Management Review*, Vol. 53. No. 3, SPRING.

Addresses the issue that innovation should not be limited to a product or a service,
but can also apply to the way the business model is set up.

Casadesus-Masanell, Ramon, and Joan E. Ricart (2011). "How to Design a Winning
Business Model", *Harvard Business Review*, Cambridge, MA, January–February
issue.

Suggests that a winning business model must be self-enhancing, and circular,
and one where improved results drive improved competitiveness of the model.

Girotra, Karan, and Serguei Netessine (2014). "Four Paths to Business Model
Innovation", *Harvard Business Review*, Cambridge, MA, July–August Issue.

Provides some practical guiding principles to achieving an innovative business
model.

Johnson, Mark W., Christensen, Clayton M., and Henning Kagermann (2008).
"Reinventing Your Business Model", *Harvard Business Review*, Cambridge,
MA, December issue.

A more generic assessment of two key issues for reinventing business models:
Understanding your current business model at granular level as well as the need
to develop a customer-focused new idea

Kim, W. Chan, and Renée Mauborgne (2005). *Blue Ocean Strategy: How to Create*
Uncontested Market Space and Make the Competition Irrelevant, Cambridge,
MA: Harvard Business School Publishing Cooperation.

A practical and insightful guide on how to develop a proposition that is new, and
that does not compete head to head in a mature market.

Porter, Michael E., and Mark R. Kramer (2011). "Creating Shared Value", *Harvard*
Business Review, Cambridge, MA, January–February issue.

A manifesto calling for creation of growth and innovation by looking at value
creation outside the strict limits of a company's activities.

Vlaar, Paul, de Vries, Paul, and Mattijs Willenborg (2005). "Why Incumbents Struggle
to Extract Value from New Strategic Options: Case of the European Airline
Industry", *European Management Journal*, Vol. 23, No. 2: pp. 154–169.

Analysis how incumbents are prone to missing disruptive new business models
in their industry as they are too attached to their current way of earning and
thus underestimate the quality required for the new.

Chapter 6: Transformation – leadership

Organizational transformation

Adler, Paul, Heckscher, Charles, and Laurence Prusak (2011). "Building a Collaborative Enterprise", *Harvard Business Review*, Cambridge, MA, July–August issue.
*Case study on how to build a collaborative organization with interdependent
knowledge-based tasks by creating a shared purpose, collaborative procedures,
and belief in diversity.*

Hamel, Gary, and Bill Breen (2007). *Building an Innovation Democracy*, Boston,
MA: Harvard Business School Press.
*An inspiring case on the innovative organization W.L. Gore used to build his
successful Gore-Tex company. (Originally published as Chapter 5 of The Future
of Management by Gary Hamel and Bill Breen).*

Kotter, John P. (2012). "Leading Change: Why Transformation Efforts Fail", *Harvard
Business Review*, Cambridge, MA, Spring issue.
*An eight-step checklist on leading organizational transformation (republished
from 1995).*

Schaffer, Robert H., and Harvey A. Thomson (1992). "Successful Change Programs
Begin with Results", *Harvard Business Review*, Cambridge, MA, January–February issue.
*Classic article on the importance of feedback from reality in any change program,
both to ensure you are on the right track and to create enthusiasm and support.*

Spear, Steven (2004). "Learning to Lead at Toyota", *Harvard Business Review*,
Cambridge, MA, May issue.
*Describes the learnings of an American organization at Toyota, especially their
leadership approach based on guiding principles rather than tools or processes.*

Genes & Memes

Dawkins, Richard ([1976] 1989). *The Selfish Gene: Oxford:* Oxford University Press.
*If you read one book on biology, it must be this one. It is not just a great study, but
an inspiration to continuously look for what drives the world in general.*

Dawkins, Richard ([1982] 2008). *The Extended Phenotype,* Oxford: Oxford University
Press.
*Expanding on his original book, Dawkins adds to the understanding by blurring
the border between an individual and its environment.*

Yochai Benkler (2011). "The Unselfish Gene", *Harvard Business Review*, Cambridge,
MA, July–August issue.
*Addresses the misconception that selfish genes mean that people will always
behave selfishly. Instead, it explains how the same biological phenomenon can
lead to altruism and other forms of socially beneficial behaviors.*

Leadership

Hassan, Fred (2011). "The Frontline Advantage", *Harvard Business Review*, Cambridge, MA, May issue.
Reflects on the importance of 'frontline' managers and, more generally, on visiting the work floor to collect insights on how to handle transformation challenges.

Olanrewaju, Tunde, Smaje, Kate, and Paul Willmott (2014). "The Seven Traits of Effective Digital Enterprises", London: McKinsey & Company.
http://www.mckinsey.com/business-functions/organization/our-insights/ the-seven-traits-of-effective-digital-enterprises
Gives the characteristics of successful digital companies.

Senge, Peter M. (1990). "The Leader's New Work: Building Learning Organizations", *Sloan Management Review*, Vol. 32, No. 1: pp. ??*
Article based on the book below.

Senge, Peter M. (1990). *The Fifth Discipline: The Art and Practices of a Learning Organization*, New York: Doubleday.
A management classic. Even if the full impact of the fifth discipline did not materialize, it is filled with great insights. Especially interesting on process thinking.

Leading through intent

Davis, Stanley M. (1982). "Transforming Organizations: The Key to Strategy is Context", *Organizational Dynamics*, Vol. 10, No. 3, Winter: p.64.
Although it starts with theory, it is a brilliant article that shows that as soon as a company has accepted its strategic intent (Context), the strategy is implemented.

Marciano, Sonia (2017). *Bigger Isn't Always Better*, New York: NYU Stern.
https://www.l2inc.com/daily-insights/bigger-isnt-always-better?utm_ source=email&utm_medium=email&utm_content=the-daily&utm_ campaign=email
Addresses the impact of concentration on business, and calls for a rebalancing of the role of business in society.

Pirsig, Robert M. (1974). *Zen and The Art of Motorcycle Maintenance: An Inquiry into Values*, New York: Harper Collins.
This book gets more interesting with repeated reading. A central and beautiful concept is the idea that real quality is to be found not in the tangible, not in the intangible, but in a combination of the two. A principle that applies to many aspects of life.

Scott, James C. (1998). *Seeing Like a State: How Certain Schemes to Improve the Human Condition Have Failed*, New Haven, CT: Yale University Press.
This book gives context on how humanity cannot force improvement though complex systems or societies and with a purely rational approach.

Smith, Charles E. (1994). "The Merlin Factor: Leadership and Strategic Intent", *Journal name?* Vol. 5, Spring: pp.???
How to approach transformation from strategic intent through co-invention, engagement, and practice.

Generic studies on ecology

Despard Estes, Richard (1991). *The Behavior Guide to African Mammals*, Berkeley, CA, University of California Press.

If you visit the African savannah and you are interested in understanding what you see, do not forget to take this book with you on safari.

Gurney, W.S.C., and R.M. Nisbet (1998). *Ecological Dynamics*, Oxford: Oxford University Press.

Good guide to better understanding techniques for modelling and understanding ecology.

Sinclair A., and M. Norton-Griffith (eds.) (1979). *Serengeti: Dynamics of an Ecosystem* Chicago: University of Chicago Press.

A collection of interesting and accessible articles on the African ecosystem.

Index

Printed and bound by CPI Group (UK) Ltd, Croydon, CR0 4YY

13/04/2025

14656554-0001